Quick Reference to

Redesigning the
Nursing Organization

4/11/96

Midge —
Best wishes for
a happy life out "west!"
St V.'s & I will miss you.
It's been great working
with you. Mary Fisher

Delmar Publishers' Online Services

To access Delmar on the World Wide Web, point your browser to:
http://www.delmar.com/delmar.html
To access through Gopher: gopher://gopher.delmar.com
(Delmar Online is part of "thomson.com", an Internet site with information on
more than 30 publishers of the International Thomson Publishing organization.)
For information on our products and services:
email: info@delmar.com
or call 800-347-7707

Quick Reference to

Redesigning the Nursing Organization

Mary L. Fisher, PhD, RN, CNAA
Associate Professor
Indiana University School of Nursing
Indianapolis, Indiana

Delmar Publishers

 An International Thomson Publishing Company

Albany • Bonn • Boston • Cincinnati • Detroit • London
Madrid • Melbourne • Mexico City • New York • Pacific Grove • Paris
San Francisco • Singapore • Tokyo • Toronto • Washington

NOTICE TO THE READER

Publisher does not warrant or guarantee any of the products described herein or perform any independent analysis in connection with any of the product information contained herein. Publisher does not assume, and expressly disclaims, any obligation to obtain and include information other than that provided to it by the manufacturer.

The reader is expressly warned to consider and adopt all safety precautions that might be indicated by the activities herein and to avoid all potential hazards. By following the instructions contained herein, the reader willingly assumes all risks in connection with such instructions.

The publisher makes no representation or warranties of any kind, including but not limited to, the warranties of fitness for particular purpose or merchantability, nor are any such representations implied with respect to the material set forth herein, and the publisher takes no responsibility with respect to such material. The publisher shall not be liable for any special, consequential, or exemplary damages resulting, in whole or part, from the readers' use of, or reliance upon, this material.

Delmar Staff
Publisher: Diane L. McOscar
Senior Acquisitions Editor: Bill Burgower
Assistant Editor: Hilary Schrauf

Project Editor: Judith Boyd Nelson
Production Coordinator: Barbara A. Bullock
Art and Design Coordinator: Carol Keohane
Cover Design: John Orozco

COPYRIGHT © 1996 By Delmar Publishers
a division of International Thomson Publishing Inc.
The ITP logo is a trademark under license.
Printed in the United States of America

For more information, contact:
Delmar Publishers
3 Columbia Circle, Box 15015
Albany, New York 12212-5015

International Thomson Publishing Europe
Berkshire House 168-173
High Holborn
London, WC1V 7AA
England

Thomas Nelson Australia
102 Dodds Street
South Melbourne, 3205
Victoria, Australia

Nelson Canada
1120 Birchmont Road
Scarborough, Ontario
Canada, M1K 5G4

International Thomson Editores
Campos Eliseos 385, Piso 7
Col Polanco
11560 Mexico D F Mexico

International Thomson Publishing GmbH
Konigswinterer Strasse 418
53227 Bonn
Germany

International Thomson Publishing Asia
221 Henderson Road
#05-10 Henderson Building
Singapore 0315

International Thomson Publishing—Japan
Hirakawacho Kyowa Building, 3F
2-2-1 Hirakawacho
Chiyoda-ku, Tokyo 102
Japan

1 2 3 4 5 6 7 8 9 10 XXX 01 00 99 98 97 96 95

Library of Congress Cataloging-in-Publication Data
Fisher, Mary L.
    Quick reference to redesigning the nursing organization / Mary L.
Fisher.
        p. cm. — (Quick reference series)
    Includes bibliographical references and index.
    ISBN 0-8273-6400-8
    1. Nursing services—Administration.   2. Organizational change.
I. Title.   II. Series: Quick reference series (Albany, N.Y.)
    [DNLM: 1. Nursing Services—organization & administration.
    2. Organizational Innovation.   3. Nurse Administrators.   4. Nursing,
    Supervisory—organization & administration. WY 105 F535q 1996]
    RT89.F536   1996
    362.1'73'068—dc20
    DNLM/DLC
    for Library of Congress
                                                                                    95-35757
                                                                                    CIP

To Joann Holt, mentor and friend, who inspired me to stretch my thinking by insisting that I explore possibilities. She introduced me to scholarly leadership, the necessity of knowing what is out there. She helped me to see that managing change ethically is our most important leadership role.

Delmar Quick Reference Series in Nursing Administration
Ruth Alward, Series Editor

Quick Reference to Nursing Leadership
Donna M. Costello-Nickitas, PhD, RN

Quick Reference to Redesigning the Nursing Organization
Mary L. Fisher, PhD, RN, CNAA

Quick Reference for Directors of Nursing in Long-Term Care
Ethel L. Mitty, EdD, RN

Introduction to the Quick Reference Series

With this book we introduce a series of quick reference volumes for the busy nurse administrator and manager. Regardless of education and experience, there are many occasions when you need to turn to a reference book in your normal workday or as you begin a new position, a new project, or a new committee assignment. Rather than having to consult more generalized nursing administration textbooks, you can now turn to books designed to be easily accessible and practical, featuring helpful tables and figures, as well as examples of approaches that work.

Each volume in the Quick Reference Series is targeted to meeting the need for pertinent information on the topics you have identified as important to your management practice. Nursing administration students will also find the series instructive.

We are committed to providing excellence in the content, format, and usability of the Quick Reference Series.

Ruth R. Alward, EdD, RN
Series Editor
President, Nurse Executive Associates, Inc.
Washington, DC

Contributors

Deborah K. Asberry, MS
Development Consultant
St. Vincent Hospital and Health Care Services
Indianapolis, Indiana

Gail Ingersoll, EdD, MSN, FAAN
Department Chairperson, Nursing Administration and Teacher Education
    and Associate Professor
Indiana University School of Nursing
Indianapolis, Indiana

Karlene M. Kerfoot, PhD, RN, CNAA, FAAN
Executive Vice President, Patient Care and Chief Nursing Officer
St. Luke's Episcopal Hospital
Houston, Texas

Jude A. Magers, MSN
Organizational Development Consultant
St. Vincent Hospital and Health Care Services
Indianapolis, Indiana

Kathryn J.Parks, MA, CPHQ
Director, Quality and Utilization Management
PrimeHealth
Mobile, Alabama

Duke Rohe, FHIMSS
Senior Management Engineer
St. Luke's Episcopal Hospital
Houston, Texas

Contents

Quick Reference Topics

List of Figures and Tables

Preface

This book is written primarily for nurse executives, nurse managers, nurse educators, and students of nursing redesign. The principles contained in this book are, however, general and can benefit anyone in a leadership position within health care. This book is about leading fundamental change. It is also about questioning assumptions in order to move beyond conventional thinking.

A systems perspective is used throughout the book to give readers a sense of the context, as well as the processes of redesign. The culture an organization presents is an underlying factor in its adaptability to innovation and change.

Quick Reference to Redesigning the Nursing Organization begins with an introduction to redesign efforts. The broad view of creating the transforming organization through establishing a culture for learning and tolerance for paradigm changes is presented. Methods to promote a passion for innovation and creativity set the stage for an environment that supports change. The political and cultural aspects of redesign begin with a discussion of ethical leadership. The need for leaders to promote synergy by employing a coherent and consistent approach within the chaotic context of change is argued.

The dynamics of change undergird the redesign process. Organizational readiness for change and structures that support change are vital to successful innovation. Change is viewed as a political process, and thus collaborative negotiation skills are highlighted.

Analyzing work flow from a customer orientation begins the process of the redesign effort. Key concepts of quality improvement theory are presented to provide readers with a framework for analysis. The end point of the analysis and decision stage is a project plan. Readers are provided a framework for project development. This section is a "how-to" approach for working through the project planning process.

Implementing is frequently the weakest part of major change initiatives. By this time, consultants have left the organization to its own devices. Many projects are hampered by poor implementation plans. Chapter 4 focuses on political, cultural, logistical, and leadership issues relative to implementation planning. The suggested planning process ensures a smooth transition for the redesign effort.

Redesign requires tremendous resources from the institution, which has a right to appreciate full returns on that investment. Whether the focus of evaluation is staff retention, patient satisfaction, cost reduction, improved communications, increased revenues, or increased professional practice, the plan must be tailored to outcomes desired by the organization. The process of establishing criteria for all redesign efforts provides a foundation for process and outcome evaluation. A model for evaluation planning is provided.

Organizational development as a discipline is introduced. The dynamics of team building, worker empowerment, shared decision making, and organizational dialogue are discussed from the organizational development perspective. How to propel redesign into second- and third-generation models is outlined.

As a *Quick Reference*, the book was written with many helpful tables and figures. Where possible, visual representation is given to illustrate key ideas. Glossary terms are highlighted in **boldface** type for easy identification. Formats for project planning and other key steps in the redesign process are offered as templates.

Special thanks go to my husband, E. A. "Bud" Fisher, for his editing expertise on the initial draft of the manuscript and his patience during the birth of this book. Thanks also are given to the people at the Medical Education Resources Department (MERP) of Indiana University/Purdue University at Indianapolis (IUPUI) for their graphics assistance for some figures and to the contributors for the chapters on the learning organization, innovation, change, analyzing work flow and organizational development.

Introduction: Taking Control of Change

This book is about skills and philosophy. We, as leaders, are bound by our attitudes and frameworks. It is impossible to realign our organizations if we cannot change our own thinking. I hope this book challenges you to do so.

Redesign must be an endless journey as our organizations become driven by a commitment to excellence (Porter-O'Grady, 1992). We must learn to tolerate ambiguity as changes become aligned to an ever-shifting vision of the future. However, health care leaders must never forget that redesign affects people through reassignment of responsibilities, changes in job descriptions, and insecurity. Part of the burden of leadership is to absorb uncertainty for our staff. This is done, in part, through calmly giving guidance and vision in a way that eliminates confusion as to the direction of change. These concepts fit nursing, as well as the larger health care organization.

The central question in redesign is: How can current practices be improved as we grapple with the certainty that change is mandated by economic and political realities? This book is positioned to serve nursing service administrators and educators in presenting an organizational framework and practical guide to redesign efforts. I hope to provide a conceptual yet practical template of the redesign process along with key skills needed for successful implementation.

Nursing has an enormous stake in controlling the direction and pace of innovation for the profession. A need to emphasize retaining professional practice within the context of redesign pressures nurse executives to provide a framework and vision of what nursing can be. Nurses must have time for the serious thinking that allows for professionalism. It is what Wilson (1992, p. 6) calls the "affective and cognitive requirements of care." This critical aspect of care may be jeopardized if a bean-counting approach to redesign focuses only on tasks that are easily discernable to MBA observers.

Leaders need key skills to direct the business of redesign. This book provides many of these and some helpful tools for the process of change. This brand of change is more inclusive than the changes many readers have previously directed. It must be process driven, or it will not work. People will not accept these fundamental changes if they are not part of the change process. There are many ways these changes can be undermined at the operational level. Leaders in ivory towers may not even know that the changes they thought were complete have eroded to previous practice levels; hence, the emphasis on implementation and ongoing evaluation.

Finally, redesign should not be undertaken merely as a way to get on the bandwagon. That wagon may not be going in your direction. Vision *must* set the course of redesign, and it may be different for every area of every organization.

REFERENCES

Porter-O'Grady, T. (1992). In C. K. Wilson (Ed.), *Building new organizations: Visions and realities*. Gaithersburg, MD: Aspen.

Wilson, C. K. (1992). *Building new organizations: Visions and realities*. Gaithersburg, MD: Aspen.

CHAPTER 1

The Learning Organization

DEBORAH K. ASBERRY AND MARY L. FISHER

Redesign is change of a fundamental nature. Coming to grips with how to manage change is vital for organizations, which must evolve with changing times in order to survive. But *how* is change accomplished? Three broad areas must transform:

- people
- systems
- technology

The difficult part of change is seeing through the surface complexities to view the underlying structures generating change (Senge, 1990). In many ways, the leader's challenge is to control the pace and targets of change while competing with the external forces that are demanding change. The concept of **leverage** may best explain this process. The best results come "not from large-scale efforts but from small well-focused actions" (Senge, 1990, p. 114) Leaders must target change to achieve the best leverage (economy) from the efforts that change requires.

Paradigms and **transformations** are the topics of the day. With all of this requirement for change, the organization must invest in its employees to ensure successful change. Not only must individuals learn new paradigms; the organization as well must be transformed into a learning organization.

THE LEARNING ORGANIZATION DEFINED

Senge (1990) identifies four basic principles in his definition of learning organizations:

- People expand their capacity to create desired results.
- New and expanded patterns of thinking are nurtured.

- Collective aspirations are set free.
- People continually learn **how** to learn together.

Garvin's (1993) definition is more action oriented: "a **learning organization** is an organization skilled at creating, acquiring, and transferring knowledge, and at modifying its behavior to reflect new knowledge and insights" (p. 80). He believes this is accomplished through five main activities:

1. systematic problem solving
2. experimentation with new approaches
3. learning from personal experience and past history
4. learning from experience and best practices of others
5. transferring knowledge quickly and efficiently through an organization

A learning organization is dynamic and always changing. Change occurs as a way of creating new approaches that resolve existing problems with a current system or as a totally new paradigm for future ventures.

When people do not learn and change, old practices often continue. Change is then cosmetic—a result of jumping on a bandwagon that has no conductor. Individuals may more easily sabotage change in an environment where old paradigms predominate.

PARADIGMS FOR CHANGE

A paradigm is a personal worldview about a concept based on historical, cultural, and/or value-driven ideals. When the term *wristwatch* is used, for example, most people envision an analogue watch with hands moving around a fulcrum. Those who have embraced the digital watch have switched paradigms about wristwatches. But even those of us who stubbornly hold on to our "real" watches may have a digital alarm clock sitting on the dresser. These small bows to innovation represent opportunity for real breakthroughs in a larger context.

Every person makes a cost-benefit analysis when it comes to change. Some quickly embrace new styles; others will never go with the crowd. It is like that in health care as well. Figure 1.1 lists some paradigms to consider in judging your organization's readiness for change.

FIGURE 1.1 Managerial Paradigm Shifts to Consider

Quantity $\longrightarrow$ Quality

Operational focus $\longrightarrow$ Customer focus

Compliance $\longrightarrow$ Commitment

Individual focus $\longrightarrow$ Team focus

Routine workers $\longrightarrow$ Knowledge workers

Detection $\longrightarrow$ Prevention

Manage $\longrightarrow$ Lead

Resist change $\longrightarrow$ Innovation

Chain of command $\longrightarrow$ Fluid organization

Focused power $\longrightarrow$ Shared decisions

End justifies means $\longrightarrow$ Ethical leadership

Another paradigm that is changing involves the very structure of bureaucracies: boundaries, which prevent quick transfer of information and isolate departments, and compartmentalization, which entrusts key activities to homogeneous groups that specialize in a specific area. Both of these structural aspects of bureaucracies result in associates' limiting their focus to narrower issues, often without regard for the greater good of the organization. Techniques to open boundaries—project teams, design teams, innovation task forces, cross-departmental meetings, and customer focus groups—allow for an infusion of new ideas and perspectives.

Within organizations, another dynamic paradigm is the nature of manager-follower relationships and roles. Table 1.1 highlights the direction of change in these relationships through role shifts that are occurring in all industries.

TABLE 1.1 Paradigm Changes for Management and Staff

	CURRENT	NEW
Management	Lead	Foster leadership in others
	Manage	Integrate and ensure resources
	Direct	Facilitate and support
	Control	Release control
	Problem solve	Arrive at mutual decisions with staff
	Conduct meetings	Develop others to lead meetings
	Do	Delegate
	Evaluate	Add peer evaluation; challenge staff aspirations
	Give orders	Build consensus; market ideas
Staff	Dependent, vocational role	Professional role
	Bring problem to manager	Solve problems; collaborate with manager
	Accept policies	Participate in writing policies; become committed to improving customer service
	Follow	Lead committees; be full participants
	Continue learning	Be accountable for competencies; mentor new staff
	Powerless	Empowered: control professional practice, standards of care

Kanter (1986) recommends approaching problems with **kaleidoscope thinking**—that is, trying to rearrange the pieces to create a new pattern. In order to find this new pattern, our assumptions must be challenged. Sovie (1986) suggests that the creativity needed to accomplish new thinking is characterized by playfulness and irreverence.

One shifting business paradigm is especially hard for Americans to accept: the trend to discount individualism while promoting a sense of community and team spirit. Americans are rugged individualists, and they have trouble subjugating their needs for a greater good. But this is exactly what business is expecting now. The trend may have begun with the growth of world competition and interdependence or the introduction of Japanese management theories. According to this new paradigm, individuals must learn new group skills and be more fully engaged in the changes that are occurring. Such learning is needed to transform organizations.

A MODEL FOR CHANGE

Leaders involved in transforming an organization need a model to guide them. Without a structure to work from, the process of change can become random and chaotic. Vision, mission, and philosophy statements all are important, but they are best realized within a context.

For a model to serve an organization well, it must be fluid, dynamic, and multidimensional, thus providing a structure that is not linear or reductionistic. Parts of the model are related and interdependent; they can be almost a mirror of how to design work. The model needs to be dynamic so that it does not become obsolete before the stage of implementation. The multidimensional aspect allows us to draw from the contemporary wisdom of many disciplines, allows us to broaden our scope of awareness, and provides richness and diversity. The model in Figure 1.2 contains three intersecting components that represent a possible context for change in the learning organization:

1. The *individual* within an organization who is involved on a personal level in the change process.

FIGURE 1.2 Model for Change

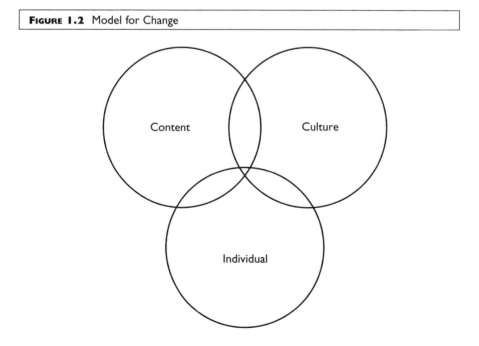

Content

Culture

Individual

Source: Courtesy of St. Vincent Health Services and Deborah Asberry.

2. The *culture* of the organization, which will be the backdrop for the change.
3. The content, including skills or new knowledge needed to facilitate the change.

Each component can be addressed in isolation; however, the synergy created as these components come together is what will propel the transformation.

AREAS FOR PERSONAL TRANSFORMATION

- **creativity**
- **personal empowerment and accountability**
- **personal mastery (lifelong learning)**
- **spirituality (meaning, soulfulness)**

The Individual

People make up systems, and so any model for change must pay attention to those whose lives are affected by it. The pace of change in health care demands that those involved in the direct delivery of care be nurtured, supported, and mentored in any change process. Harman and Hormann (1990) talk about creativity in the workplace: "Fundamentally we work to create, and only incidentally do we work to eat" (p. 26). Rigid policy, autocratic forms of governance, and performance appraisal based on compliance have quite successfully driven out any place for creativity in most work sites. Corporate success demands that we create work environments that promote creativity, openness, and tolerance for change.

Training and staff development therefore must include components of empowerment and personal growth. Inherent in this work is the idea of personal accountability. Empowerment and accountability are strangers in our work world, especially in nonmanagement areas. The rank and file traditionally function from a paradigm of helplessness and blame.

TIP

We must provide work environments that do not demand that associates park their brains at the door.

Much individual work must be done as we go about transforming an organization. Personal transformation propels organizational change. Without it, we shift and turn but basically stay the same.

The work of personal empowerment takes many forms. An organization can hire a consultant firm that specializes in empowerment training. The model can serve as the context of this training to ensure follow-up and application within the organization. A train-the-trainer model could be implemented to minimize costs and the need to send large groups of staff to workshops and training sessions. Whatever the form chosen, the individual must be supported in the change process and invited into the journey on both an individual and an organizational level. Senge (1990) points out four benefits that occur as people begin the journey of empowerment and lifelong learning:

1. We become adept at sharpening our own personal visions.
2. We broaden our perspective of reality.
3. We increase awareness of our biases and assumptions.
4. We bring meaning into our work lives.

We therefore must support the continued growth and development of each individual.

Another aspect of individual support that is receiving renewed attention is the spiritual component. David Whyte, in his book *The Heart Aroused*, is one of many contemporary authors who focus on the spiritual dimension in business today. Since Descartes uttered the famous words, "I think therefore I am," our souls have been progressively left behind as we have come to deify logic. Aesthetics, passion, grief, fear, and love have been suspect in the workplace. We have operated from a myth that soul and mind must be separated, especially at work. In this Faustian bargain, we have workers whose daily guide is the day planner. As we think about soul or the lack of soul in our organizations, it should bring us to our knees. People who come to work without a soulfulness or a sense of meaning are not open to change. They will merely mouth the words, but change will not get inside their bodies. People who are not engaged in the work that they do but are merely there to get a paycheck will fear anything that looks like change. The fear will be from a deep place of security and safety. "Our work life, reduced to ashes without the fuel of our deep personal desires, becomes an unconscious way to commit suicide," writes David Whyte (1994, p. 265). Organizational transformation is a spiritual journey. The organization that understands this will survive.

Culture

The cultural component of the model focuses on the beliefs, assumptions, rules, and rituals that determine the performance of the collective. Culture for the most part lies just below the level of consciousness, yet corporate culture dictates our behaviors and attitudes. We are not always aware of nor do we have language to think about the culture. Usually the words that we do have explain only the observable, the surface level of the culture. Organizational change must include an accurate assessment of the culture, and give voice and structure to the new culture that will emerge from the change process. Because of the importance of culture in the redesign process, Chapter 3 is devoted to an in-depth discussion of culture.

> ### TIP
>
> The merging of hospitals with other health care systems, the purchase of physician practices by third-party payors, and the emergence of shared decision-making models of governance are examples of a cultural shift from autocratic, top-down forms of governance (**patriarchy**) to forms of collaboration and cooperation (**partnership**).

As cultural issues are discussed, it is helpful to look at the societal changes that are occurring in the culture and begin to use the words that have emerged from this work. Peter Block discusses the paradigm shift from patriarchy to partnership in his book, *Stewardship*. The dilemma is that we know implicitly the rules of patriarchy but do not have much knowledge about partnership. Therefore, the changes that occur in forms of governance may be in word only until we become conscious of the rules of both. Figure 1.3 sets out some differences between patriarchy and partnership.

Cultural emphasis should include discussions and readings that bring to the light these two paradigms. People within organizations need to understand how cultures change and the time needed for change to occur. Cultural change is not an absolute process whereby we walk out a door of patriarchy and enter the house of partnership. The road is slippery, and we may trip along the way.

In this process of change, it may seem as though the organization is sending mixed messages and is insincere about its desire for new ways of work-

FIGURE 1.3 Rules of Patriarchy and Partnership	
RULES OF PATRIARCHY	**RULES OF PARTNERSHIP**
• Submit to authority	• All responsible for vision
• Deny self-expression	• All responsible for environment
• Sacrifice (for something)	• All responsible for feelings

ing. Shared governance is a perfect example of how the patriarchy and partnership can bump into each other. For example, councils may be given permission to develop policy about schedules, pay, and benefits, yet a corporate dictate may then be handed down contradicting a new policy developed in a council. Unless there is understanding and compassion for the old bumping into the new, resentment, cynicism, and low morale may develop. The scope of partnership therefore must be clarified. If there are constraints or limitations to the governance model, the boundaries should be made as clear as possible.

Leaders play a pivotal role in changing an organizational culture. Their leadership style either supports the old controlling paradigm of patriarchy, which demands predictability and compliance, or encourages a workplace of creativity, **empowerment**, and change. The leaders who understand their new role are not afraid of losing their power in the process. They begin to govern from a place of vision, authenticity, and wisdom. Leaders are needed in both paradigms; the role of leadership is the fundamental difference between them. As leaders step into their new role, they begin to change the culture and invite others to do so with them.

EXAMPLES OF ASSUMPTIONS AND BELIEFS THAT MUST BE QUESTIONED

- **The quieter the patient is, the easier it is to deal with him or her.**
- **The more expensive the procedure, the more accurate it is.**
- **If cost is reduced, quality suffers.**
- **Paperwork is not as important as bedside care.**
- **We do not hold peers accountable for practice; it would not be "nice."**
- **All caregivers are equal because they can do the same tasks.**

> **TIP**
>
> Cultural assessment is a journey of consciousness. The assumptions and beliefs of an organization must be uncovered. The more conscious we become of the assumptions, the less power they have over our behavior and emotions.

This list of assumptions was discovered as a part of cross-training for patient-focused care. These assumptions determined the amount of acceptance or resistance to the patient-focused redesign process. Training absolutely had to consider culture. Only then were staff able to enter into dialogue about how they reacted to a patient in acute pain, the resentment felt toward a team leader who took time to do paperwork, and cost reduction on the unit. Once the assumptions were brought to the fore, the group could begin to work toward a collective definition of how they wanted the unit to function.

Models for organizational change must include attention to the culture. Consciousness of the assumptions and beliefs of the old culture must be uncovered, and words given that begin to describe the emerging culture. Patience is called for as the old culture begins to fade and the new begins to take form. As leaders become conscious of their patterns of behaviors that supported the old culture and begin to change their own beliefs and assumptions, they model that process for others. It is that simple—and it is that hard.

Content

The third dimension of the model speaks to the content inherent in supporting the changing culture. It should be obvious by now that this is not a linear, sequential model but that each dimension parallels and includes the others. As the individual is supported in personal growth, empowerment, and accountability, there are certain skills and knowledge to be gained, that support changing the culture. All are interdependent.

What to teach as we attempt to change an organization is a provocative question. If part of the cultural change is the shifting of roles from task to process, all teaching should reflect that as well. However, much training that occurs across the country is actually a broadening of the tasks for staff to accomplish. There has been an almost universal outcry that what is being expected from staff is more work for less money. Staff feel betrayed, belittled, and angry. These emotions usually are not outwardly and authentically expressed but emerge in the form of sabotage and low morale.

It seems as though we have a paradox: To orchestrate a change of culture, we need to redefine practice. As we redefine practice, we broaden areas of accountability and decision making. This all looks good in theory, but it feels a lot like more for less. What is missing?

Inherent in a changing culture is a change of relationship. We must begin to relate to each other differently. These relationships take many forms, including the creation of primary care teams, councils, and collaborative ventures. Our old way of looking at the world would suggest that the skills needed to perform in these relationships are assertiveness, conflict resolution, delegation, dialogue, and team building. However, these skills are being superimposed on an old structure of relationship—one of rugged individualism, competition, and fear. We are used to relating to each other using dependency, compliance, and general mistrust of leaders. Content now needs to reflect issues of relationship, partnership, and consciousness. These are not the typical bill of fare for educational training. Competence in culture, change, and **organizational dialogue** are needed. Training must invite staff into an awakening of their own personal myths, consciousness about their own needs of security and safety, and new ways of being together in conversation where the dialogue occurs at an adult to adult level. The goal is for new learning and mutual understanding. Examples of myths needing exploration include themes of power and control, dominance and submissiveness, and distinction of self versus role. Training should be directed to all levels of the organization, from the CEO to housekeeping.

A discipline that is receiving a lot of attention in organizations is **dialogue**. Peter Senge and his colleagues are strong proponents of the value of dialogue to a learning organization and as a support for organizational change. Experiences that make explicit dialogue involving real issues have a profound effect on how people relate to one another. Training in dialogue is multidimensional. It can occur in a classroom as part of cross-training for point-of-care delivery, but it also needs to be modeled and supported on the unit, at the bedside, and in department meetings. Dialogue becomes a personal choice of relating authentically, courageously, and in real time with colleagues and patients. It is clarity about what matters most. Dialogue becomes a behavior and cultural norm that speeds transformation.

Teaching should include systems theory in order to awaken us to our interconnectedness and interdependence. Simulation experiences emphasizing the difference between fragmented and interconnected systems have proven successful and enlightening.

Training also should explore interpersonal issues of trust, power, and control. This training should be multidimensional so that it occurs both apart from and at the work site. Initially, facilitators or educators present the material, but soon the mentoring and facilitation become the work of organization leaders, both formal and informal. Personal integration of the work of trust, power, and control becomes a life perspective originating from a change in worldview. The individual begins to make a fundamental shift in relationships centered around distrust, control, and dependency to relationships of trust, service, and influence. This too is a journey of consciousness and has a spiritual component. People with positive beliefs refuse to engage in negative aspects of the organization's culture and begin to model more empowering interactions.

The initial content for instruction to support organizational change should include:

- critical thinking
- dialogue
- systems theory
- trust
- control and dependency

The scope and depth of the instruction vary with the group and the degree of change. However, these initial process-oriented topics should be a priori to the work of tasks and content. If outside consultants are asked to facilitate this training, it must be contextualized within the model so that individual content areas are given a context that imparts meaning and relevance to the training. Traditional training is fragmented and fills the hours of the day. The scope must become broader, and everything that is presented to staff should be within a meaningful context, explicit to the trainer and the trainee.

METHODOLOGY

As we attempt to become conscious as an organization—conscious of our assumptions, beliefs, and the cultural context of our behavior—we should turn to the wisdom of the ages. Poetry, literature, and symbols are keys to the unconscious and powerful teaching tools. This work of organizational change is not imparted only by overheads, flipcharts, and handouts. For example, inviting discussion after reading Plato's "Allegory of a Cave" in *The Republic* elicited an emotional discussion among nurses on a cardiac medical unit as they discussed the chains of perceptions that limited them. The use of a Zulu folk tale with a group of RNs, LPNs, and technicians opened a lively discussion of racism, sexism, and power on the unit and how they dominate relationships. Anton Chekhov's *A Nincompoop* was discussed by staff in relation to power and patriarchy. Good literature has proved to be a very cost-effective teaching tool. The learning transcends the moment in the classroom and invites soul back into organizations. This teaching approach requires a leap of faith and a facilitator with strong group dynamics skills.

In support of the learning process and consistent with becoming a learning organization, training needs to be ongoing. The traditional design of staff development in-service and training modules no longer serves us. The initial experiences in learning about dialogue, culture, and empowerment as well as the training in phlebotomy and electrocardiograms may be in a classroom, but that should be just the beginning. Continual support and amplification of the material also needs to occur in the work environment. Formal and informal leaders should begin to take on the roles of mentor, facilitator, **mediator**, and partner in living the work. The development of continued educational support should be identified by the staff as they manage their own learning.

Organizational developmental consultants at one midwestern Catholic hospital are putting on lab coats and shadowing staff as they coach them in empowerment and dialogue. Working as partners engaged in actual experiences, teacher and student find that their relationship is completely reciprocal. The learning and authentic application of skill and knowledge provide a transcendence of learning experience and a foster relationship of mutual trust. This time of confirmed application is when the light bulb really turns on and confidence in new skills is cemented.

Summary

Our model suggests that if you pay attention to the individual, notice the culture, and present the content within a meaningful context, the organization will change. People change organizations. The model presented will help people to discover their voice, find their legs, and create the work that they want.

We sound a note of caution. In Greek mythology, it was written that when the gods wanted to seek revenge on mortals, they would grant them their wishes. Our organizations were founded primarily in patriarchy, and patriarchy is alive and well in most of them. Patriarchy does not like conscious and empowered staff. If we can make it through the revolution, the phoenix that will rise from the ashes will be something to behold. It will be the organization for which we all would like to work.

References
Block, P. (1993). *Stewardship: Choosing service over self interest.* San Francisco: Berrett-Koehler.

Chekhov, A. (1960). *A Nincompoop. Anton Chekhov: Selected Stories.* New York: Penguin Group.

Garvin, D. A. (1993, July–August). Building a learning organization. *Harvard Business Review,* 78–91.

Harman, W., & Hormann, J. (1990). *Creative work.* Indianapolis, IN: Institute of Noetic Sciences.

Isaacs, W. (1993). Taking flight: Dialogue, collective thinking and organizational learning. *Organizational Dynamics.*

Kanter, R. M. (1986). *The change masters: Innovation and entrepreneurship in the American corporation.* New York: Simon & Schuster.

Peck, M. S. (1993). *A world waiting to be born: Rediscovering civility.* New York: Bantam Books.

Plato (1979). *Plato's Republic: Book 7.* Translated by G.M. Grube. Indianapolis: Hackett Pub. Co.

Senge, P. (1990). *The fifth discipline: The art and practice of the learning organization.* Garden City, NY: Doubleday.

Sovie, M. D. (1986). Doing things differently and better. *Nursing Economics,* 4(4), 201–203.

Whyte, D. (1994). *The heart aroused: Poetry and the preservation of the soul in corporate America.* Garden City, NY: Doubleday.

CHAPTER 2

A Passion for Innovation:

The St. Luke's Experience

KARLENE KERFOOT AND DUKE ROHE

Traditionally, hospitals and health care facilities have failed to see **innovation** in managerial and clinical processes as an integral part of their existence. Instead, most of the innovations that caregivers apply in care delivery have come from vendors or researchers in academia. Yet if hospitals and providers are going to respond quickly and effectively to dramatic changes in the health care market, they must turn tradition upside down and quickly redesign nursing organizations to meet new challenges.

Basic to developing innovative organizations is the building of a culture with a passion for innovation. Nurses have not been socialized to believe that innovation is part of their job. On the contrary, they have been socialized to be very cautious and to base their practice on *proven* information. Their socialization has come from schools of nursing and hospitals with highly bureaucratic, controlling environments. It is no wonder that innovation is not part of the nursing culture. However, it must become a part very quickly if nurses are to play a role in the integrated health care networks that mark a new era of health care.

TIP

The innovative culture:
- sees change as positive.
- is willing to fight for the "little" idea.
- provides resources to make change happen.

Finding New Models

Hospitals and health care facilities have little history of innovation so must look to other businesses for models of innovations, such as those in California's Silicone Valley. The registered nurse, so essential to health care's future, would be well advised to learn how innovative companies carry out their work and apply their principles to the challenges in health care.

TIP

Model: Mazda of America Mazda's leaders believe that if a procedure has not been changed for improvement in six weeks, something is wrong.

Tom Peters, in *Liberation Management* (1992), points out that "to survive for the long haul, you must passionately pursue the destruction of what you have created" (p. 489). For those who have been successful in delivering health care, it is very hard to destroy a creation in pursuit of something else— even something better.

Innovative companies such as Sony purposely plan new products to make their current ones obsolete. Hospitals and health care facilities must take that approach too, continually changing processes and procedures to make them more efficient and to deliver better-quality care. We traditionally wait for someone to call attention to the fact that we need to change, rather than being proactive as Sony has been and have a program in place to improve all current procedures and processes. Much of learning to work in an innovative structure revolves around one's ability to develop a love of perceiving, tolerating, and working with chaos.

TIP

Model: A Large Retail Chain in Texas The president of the company had just one criticism of his top engineer: he wasn't making enough mistakes.

James Gleick, in his book *Chaos* (1987), illustrates how very small changes in systems can bring about very large effects in the future. Those wanting to redesign a nursing organization should be familiar with Gleick's work because it is a solid foundation on which to base the work of innovation. They should also look at how other cultures view and implement innovation. Shigeo Shingo, in *The Sayings of Shigeo Shingo: Key Strategies for Plant Improvement* (1987), for example, applies unorthodox and flexible thinking to produce innovation.

Shingo gives an account of a company whose workers made mistakes inserting items in circuit boards. The plant was brightly lit from above, and the manager was asked the purpose of the lighting scheme. He replied that the workers needed to distinguish between various parts and insert pins in tiny holes on the circuit boards. Only moderate light from above was required to distinguish the parts, but what workers lacked was light from below to make the holes in the circuit boards plainly visible—like those in a child's Lite-brite. Once illumination masks corresponding to the parts needed in each board were created, the rate of insertion errors fell to zero. The key was to consider the purpose of illumination and then devise lighting that corresponded to the goals of the task at hand.

TIP

A checklist would be unnecessary if people never forgot, but they do. Nagging people to "be careful" or "pay attention" does not help. A checklist does. It reminds people of old information, freeing them to discover the new.

One can spark innovation within any organization, whether it has a track record of prior innovation or not. When the first author arrived at St. Luke's, Houston, Texas, she was impressed to see a large poster hanging in a nursing conference room proclaiming "Excellence Through Innovation" and assumed this must be the slogan or mission of the hospital. Certainly with Dr. Denton Cooley's milestone achievements in cardiovascular surgery, commitment to innovation seemed in keeping with the hospital's tradition, so she took up the gauntlet of innovation—only later to discover that Excellence Through Innovation was a short-lived internal campaign. There were pockets of innovation here and there, but St. Luke's had a long way to go to become truly an innovative institution.

Innovation here was far from an overnight event. Instead, it evolved through several stages, beginning with primary nursing and shared governance and leading to a current stage—not a final stage—of shared leadership. St. Luke's nursing innovation model is shown in Figure 2.1.

Figure 2.1 St. Luke's Innovation Model

Instituting **shared governance** was an important step along the way toward innovation. Under the old system, as in many other hospitals, the emphasis was on asking permission. Under shared governance, individuals are given accountability for certain areas and expected to come up with innovative ideas.

Shared leadership takes shared governance beyond the nursing department into all areas of patient care. Now shared governance meetings include respiratory therapists. The group practice meetings held by outcomes management teams include all members of the care team. Instead of a nursing quality care council, there are patient quality care councils, with nurses and pharmacists exchanging ideas rather than meeting separately.

TIP

Give in on issues that the group feels strongly about. Announce your goal as reality—and watch it become one.

FOSTERING CREATIVITY

Creativity thrives in supportive cultures and dies in unsupportive ones. Since nurses have not been socialized in innovative structures, it is useful to determine how a culture of creativity can be developed at a particular health care facility and become the basis for redesign efforts. Without creativity, redesign becomes merely a rubber stamp of someone else's program, not a creation custom-made to particular needs. (See "How to Stimulate Innovation.")

HOW TO STIMULATE INNOVATION

- Encourage low-risk change across departmental lines.
- Give staff concrete innovation tools.
- Celebrate failures and good tries as well as successes.
- Champion those individuals brave enough to be first to innovate.
- Protect the oddballs who bring different perspectives to the group.
- Repeat, repeat, repeat the innovation message.

In every culture, people behave as they are rewarded and sanctioned to behave. Creative cultures reward creative ideas, and people who foster creativity are the champions of the organization. These people become the proselytizers and the role models for a culture that supports innovation.

Members of an organization take their lead from those who model expected behaviors within the organization. The job of the chief nursing officer, the management team, and staff nurse leaders is to model creativity and innovation and reward it in everyone around them. By championing people who are innovative and ensuring that they are on center stage in leadership positions, members of the organization soon learn what is expected from them and what kinds of behaviors are rewarded.

TIP

Digout is the Japanese term for a manager who helps staff find improvements that will make their jobs easier.

An important part of creating a culture of innovation is retaining the most creative people within the culture. Unfortunately, innovative people do not fit perfectly in most models used today, and they are often drummed out of nursing organizations. Yet these are the very people needed within the ranks, because they view the world from a unique perspective important to nursing's long-term viability. One of the challenges of the manager and the chief nursing officer is to ensure that the oddballs, the zany people, and the mavericks are retained and that their creativity is channeled effectively within the organization. It was a creative nurse who developed the idea of placing pictures of Texas around her unit to make patients' walking exercise more interesting. Each picture and accompanying description helped take patients' minds off their pain.

All too often, these people leave, set up businesses of their own, and achieve success in areas they were not allowed to pursue within the organization. Creative people do not always fit the model—and they should not. It is the job of leaders to create cultures in which **diversity** is valued, where all people do not look alike and act alike, and where people who are different are valued and honored.

Managers must learn certain skills in order to carry out their key role in fostering creativity. They have traditionally been taught to manage, not to lead. They have been rewarded for keeping a lid on things and for making sure that policies and procedures are adhered to, not questioned. Managers must reengineer themselves to manage differently within a culture of innovation.

THE MANAGER'S ROLE IN INNOVATION

- **Be an innovator the staff can observe.**
- **Help staff find ways to make their jobs easier.**
- **Keep a petty-cash account for testing staff ideas.**
- **Allow mistakes.**
- **Support a staff idea from beginning through implementation.**

LISTENING AND COMMUNICATING

It is impossible to overcommunicate a vision of innovation and creativity within an organization. Many vehicles are available for these kinds of communications; forums (including open forums with staff), town hall meetings, and weekly newsletters all serve to position the organization as one that supports innovation.

At St. Luke's, two vehicles were especially useful in communicating a spirit of innovation. The first was the weekly nursing newsletter, *Nursing Update*, which featured a regular column from the executive vice president of nursing. Called "Kerfoot's Korner," this regular column was a combination of pep talk, gleanings from the latest books in the field, and updates on innovations taking place within the institution. The central message of the column, expressed in as many variations as possible, was, "We're excited and supportive of the innovations our nurses are making here." Presenting the main idea in many variations meant that staff could not miss it or forget it.

The second vehicle was a news and feature magazine created in 1990 by the nursing department with help from the hospital's editorial staff: the

Innovator. Appropriately named, the magazine swiftly became the place to highlight advances, collaborative efforts, cost savings, and other aspects of nursing innovations. The publication achieved its goals both within the hospital and outside its doors. For staff, it raised morale, generated excitement, and gave deserved recognition. To outside nursing colleagues and interested laypeople, it disseminated ideas others could implement and raised generous support for new nursing programs.

Separate but related to these communication vehicles was the development of St. Luke's Center for Innovation, which became not only the home of the *Innovator* but the originator of numerous outreach and consultation services to offer nursing colleagues and institutions. Through the center, seminars were sponsored, information about programs was disseminated, and colleagues visited to learn how to apply the innovations at their own institutions.

Much of what needs to be communicated is a culture of optimism. Peter Drucker (1985) wrote, " 'The glass is half-full' and 'the glass is half-empty' are descriptions of the same phenomenon but have vastly different meanings. Changing a manager's perception of a glass from half-empty to half-full opens up big innovation opportunities" (p. 71). Innovative cultures are optimistic ones. Quinn (1985, p. 80) points to the atmosphere and the "opportunity orientation" of innovative cultures as offering an explanation for how innovation succeeds in some places and fails in others.

TIP

Do not put up that sign reminding staff to "Eliminate Waste." If they recognized waste, they would get rid of it. Inspire staff with a new sign: "Find Waste."

Conventional wisdom is that health care organizations that listen to customers will be innovative and will adapt quickly to meet the customers' needs. However, that idea misses a key point about an innovative culture. Organizations that foster creativity do not ask customers what they need. Rather, they listen to customers' problems and issues and then design programs that address the needs customers could not articulate. True innovation does not start with what the customer wants. It abstracts from the issues customers raise and leapfrogs to what customers cannot even imagine wanting (Dumaine, 1991).

TIP

To reap full benefit from an innovation, move it from an optional to a "must" status.

TOOLS FOR INNOVATION

Creativity can and must be taught. When determining how to build a culture of innovation, certain didactic information must be taught and certain mindsets must be changed. For example, St. Luke's Episcopal Hospital started an initial redesign effort with the concept of Super Units in 1987. At that time, units were asked to wipe the slate clean of everything they had known about how a nursing unit should run and instead provide useful suggestions for how the units could be redesigned for quality and efficiency. Once these suggestions were tested in an accelerated fashion on the Super Unit, the ideas that were successful were made available to other units to adopt.

Basic to innovating is the Japanese concept of *Kaizen* (Imai, 1986). It means small improvements that save only a few minutes here and there but amount to untold hours of reduced frustration. Figure 2.2 demonstrates major factors about *Kaizen*.

FIGURE 2.2 Characteristics of *Kaizen*

Kaizen works everywhere. A nurse in the operating room was frustrated that the trash bag came loose from the hamper every time she threw in a few items. After unsuccessfully trying to order a different size bag to fit more tightly over the hamper, she came up with the *Kaizen* of ordering an industrial-size rubber band that fits around the lip of the hamper.

Obstetric staff members made a list of the 20 most frequently called telephone extensions, laminated it, and clipped it behind their identification badges. Individual members may save only seconds from thumbing through a telephone directory, but the savings add up. Another *Kaizen* came from a unit secretary who wondered why she had to unpad the many forms coming to the unit. Why couldn't they be delivered in single sheets from the print shop? This question changed the print shop's practice from padding forms to sending them individually in shrink-wrapped packages.

Also basic to innovation is the ability to see old things from a new perspective—what we call "seeing anew." Looking for improvement works in much the same manner as looking at a **holusion**, a multilayered, three-dimensional picture. You do not initially see the picture because you do not know how to look for it. Once you do understand, a new world opens.

The holusion in Figure 2.3 is an analogy to illustrate the hidden waste that lies in hospitals today. It may not look like waste—but the greatest waste is the waste we do not see. If we can begin looking at our work environment in the way we can look at this holusion, a world of changeable improvement opportunities will open.

Look at the holusion holding the page about 12 inches away. Stare at the two dark squares at the top. Slowly bring the sheet closer to your face until eventually your eyes defocus, and you see three squares. Then glance down to see several shapes stand out from the rest. If you don't see this three-dimensional image at first, do not be too disappointed: 70 percent of those who try do not see it initially. Let a friend try, and once you see that person's excitement, you'll want to try again.

Looking for improvement works in the same way. If we can look at work processes from a different angle, we will see clear ways to correct problems that recur and cause waste and frustration. Sometimes the problem and answer are obvious; sometimes they are not, and we must relentlessly search for the answer. Often the excitement of others provides us with new energy to continue the search, but ultimately we, our customers, and our hospitals are the beneficiaries of the effort.

We also used many concepts from Japanese management and taught the staff how suggestions were valued by Japanese but not American management (Japan Human Relations Association Staff, 1992).

Figure 2.3 Holusion: A Visioning Perspective

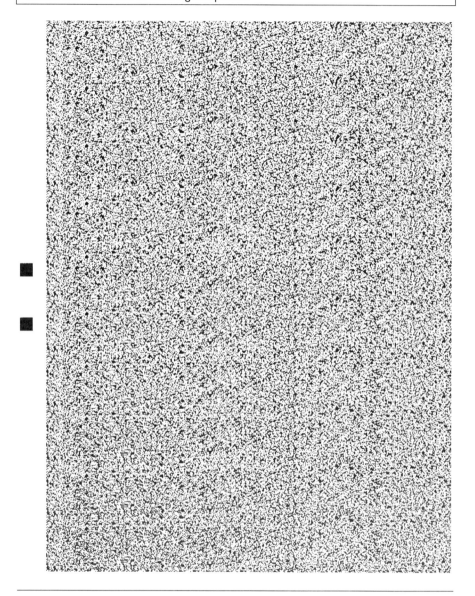

Source: Courtesy of the National Stereoscopic Association and Sol Steinberg.

JAPANESE VERSUS AMERICAN PROPOSALS, 1989

- Japanese employees averaged 36 proposals per year—a 75 percent participation rate, with 87 percent of proposals adopted.
- An American employee averages 1 proposal every 8 years—a 9 percent participation rate, with 32 percent of proposals adopted.

We looked at the life value of a lost idea. Someone whose idea is rejected or neglected may not try again, and a potential loss of 20 or 30 ideas during that person's employment will result—potentially leading to thousands of dollars lost.

To train staff members how to innovate, we taught many concrete tools and techniques, among them, quick changeover, visual control, the pocket card, and brainwriting.

Quick Changeover

Have you ever watched a car race and wondered how a car can drive into the pit, have its tires changed, windows washed, and gas tank filled in under 20 seconds? This process is called *quick changeover*, and it is accomplished by identifying which steps of the operation are external to the pit stop system and which are internal. Those that are external can be prepared ahead of time or preset for the most efficient order. Those that are internal must be performed at the time of the pit stop. Using this process, the Japanese have been able to reduce expensive machine setup times from 4 hours to 2 minutes.

A health care example is the preparation needed for receiving postoperative surgical patients in the cardiovascular intensive care unit. Internal to the system is the critical hook-up and stabilization of the patients as they come to the floor. Among the aspects that can be made external to the system are securing the suction equipment, IV poles, adjusting furniture, assembling forms, and even having the forms stacked in the order in which they are to be filled out. Every minute and every thought that is made external to the system reduces the time it takes to stabilize the patient.

Visual Control

This method uses color, pictures, and signs to help reduce waste or error or to help an employee do the job right. It was tried in the operating room, where a 3- to 5-minute scrub is required. To help scrubbers pass the time, nurses installed acrylic plastic frames to hold information about new products and new procedures for the staff and doctors to see and read every morning.

FIGURE 2.4 No Food and Drink Label

Another successful example of visual control is the 1-inch removable adhesive "no food and drink" label (Figure 2.4) sized to fit on the headboard or room number plate. Developed by a nurse who works with international patients, the label visually communicates the restriction, helping staff, patients, and guests comply. The essence of visual control is to make the instruction self-evident—and these labels certainly accomplish that goal.

The Pocket Card

Ideas for improvement need to be captured while they are fresh. The pocket-sized card (Figure 2.5) is ideal for capturing ideas that come to the staff throughout the day. In fact, the size of the card was an improvement from a staff member who claimed she always forgot her idea as she went to her locker for a standard size sheet of paper—the original size introduced. The reverse side of the card stimulates idea generation by asking, "Did you have a problem?" and "Is there something you don't like?" A nurse may not reveal a "problem"—because she or he worked double time to overcome it—but will specify what she or he did not like about the obstacle.

Brainwriting

A method of stimulating idea generation, brainwriting can result in a new idea every 30 seconds. This is accomplished by dividing staff into groups of five with a chair or table in the center of each group. A problem is defined, and each group member quickly tries to write three ideas on his or her brainwriting sheet (Figure 2.6). Members set their sheets down in the middle of the

FIGURE 2.5 Pocket Idea Card

IDEA CARD
FOR COMMUNICATING IMPROVEMENTS

NAME: _____

Title: _____ Unit: _____

Ext: _____ Date: _____

Capture your idea before it gets cold. Use this pocket card to jot down a problem you want fixed, or a solution you want to test. Best results come from those within your control, however, all ideas are appreciated.

Problem (What you don't like):

Solution (How to fix it):

Estimated Savings (optional):
_____ Min. x _____ Occurrences / day =
_____ Min./ day–week

Flow: Idea > Unit Manager > VP >
Improvement Committee

group as soon as they finish writing the three ideas, then pick up someone else's sheet and add another three ideas to the ones already there. Humor and zany ideas—but no repetition—are allowed. In 3 minutes, a group of five generates about 30 ideas. This method is less threatening than brainstorming, forces ideas out, promotes participation by the quiet members, and dispels the myth that ideas are limited to the gifted few.

FIGURE 2.6   Brainwriting Worksheet

Brainwriting Worksheet

OBSTACLE	
#	Description

1a	1b	1c
2a	2b	2c
3a	3b	3c
4a	4b	4c
5a	5b	5c

Source: Reprinted with permission from Gary Starke (1995) *Reengineering Implementation Toolkit.* Holland and Davis.

Programs

In addition to specific strategies, active programs to change the culture were implemented. Supporting all ideas and ensuring that there is no such thing as a bad idea was one way of helping people to be more confident in providing new information. We also changed the language. We took out negative words such as *problems* and *barriers*, and replaced them with *challenges*, *opportunities*, and similar other terms. When the language of optimism is used, behaviors will also change. We also encouraged people to use others' ideas and improve upon them, noting that the greatest compliment is having your own idea used and improved on. By doing this, the group owned the idea rather than having it stop with individual ownership.

BUILDING TEAMWORK IN ORGANIZATIONS OF INNOVATION

Innovation requires that people from diverse cultures, departments, and professions come together to create new models for the future. Furthermore, innovation requires that people who are very different work together in highly synergized teams. Therefore, being able to work in integrated, cross-functional, and heterogeneous teams is a requirement for organizations of innovation.

TIP

There are four goals of innovation:
1. Make things easier.
2. Make things better.
3. Make things faster.
4. Make things cheaper.

In traditional organizations, synergized, self-managed teams are not the norm. Often people lack a sense of bonding, belonging, and really owning their work. Since they are not committed to the work, their coworkers, or the organization, they have no sense that they are a valued member of the organization or that their output is important. The more we can break organizations into small, self-managed work groups, the more innovation we can stimulate. Moreover, because isolated teams do not achieve innovation, we need to ensure that project teams have many networking opportunities so that they can learn from other people's ideas and their ideas can be cross-fertilized into other teams and other units. It is possible for innovation to come out of one person working alone; however, it flourishes when diverse minds get together and exchange information unavailable to those socialized in an authoritarian model of health care.

TWO PARADOXES OF INNOVATION

- **The worst idea is the one that is not shared.**
- **It is what you do now—when you do not have to do anything— that makes you what you want to be when it is too late to do anything about it.**

Teams, however, do not run by themselves, and knowing how to work in teams is not innate. At St. Luke's Episcopal Hospital, we worked our second-generation reengineering around a patient-first care innovation called TeamCare. As part of the inculturation for this patient-focused philosophy, we taught conflict resolution, negotiation skills, listening, and communications techniques so people would have clear, useable knowledge about how to work together as teams. It is interesting that many people who participated in this orientation revealed unsolicited information about how this training had changed their lives at home, their social lives, and the level of their interactions with others. We cannot assume that people understand teams and teamwork. We must provide didactic and experiential learning experiences for them to be able to work together in teams.

Manion (1993) points out that innovation can result in chaos or transformation and offers five steps for managing innovation:

1. preparation
2. movement
3. team creativity
4. new reality
5. integration

Health care needs transformation and can do with less chaos, although chaos is unavoidable in this era. By thoughtfully working with these stages, however, better outcomes will result. She describes the team creativity phase as solving issues of "priority setting, climate developing, coordination, cooperation, team building and networking, and internal communications" (p. 46). Managers who use this model can help guide both the development of an innovative culture and specific innovations. Such development entails moving from a bureaucratic, hierarchical organization to one that fosters entrepreneurial spirit and empowered partnerships among people on the front lines and management. Under these conditions, ideas flourish and innovations abound.

We do have a word of caution: in some self-managed, synergized teams, **group-think** can become a problem that stifles initiative. Group-think occurs when the group becomes so tightly bonded that members refrain from disagreeing out of fear of ostracism from the group (Janis, 1982). Harvey well articulates the process of group-think in his book, *The Abilene Paradox* (1988). He points out that after a failure, people often say that they knew that it would not work in the first place but that they were afraid to disagree with the group. Innovation can be killed in organizations that become self-serving and synergized beyond the ability to permit and support differences of opinion.

PERMITTING FAILURE: WHY RISK IS VITAL

Innovations thrive where failure is applauded and supported. When we were carrying out the Super Unit and TeamCare redesigns, an important underpinning of these projects was the celebration of failure. Nurses are socialized to believe that because failure leads to death, no failures can be allowed. They can be freed to innovate with many procedures that, rather than causing death, are very safe to think about improving.

Peters (1992) maintains that in order to embrace success, one must embrace failure. People learn from their mistakes and go on to build even better ideas. More than that, a culture of innovation thoroughly understands that not every effort is going to be a hit. Many successes are serendipitous offshoots of projects that failed. If organizations are not failing, they are not trying. They are stifling initiative, allowing only ideas that are sure bets for success to generate. However, if people can learn to try, to fail, and to try again, they learn to wade through uncharted waters and become innovative in new and different ways than they had thought of before. In Tom Peters's (1992) words, the essence of success is failure.

TIP

Find problems where you think none exist.

SUMMARY

Innovative cultures develop out of passion. Innovation thrives in organizations where it is rewarded, sought after, and celebrated. It dies when failure is feared and punishment follows imperfection. This does not mean that innovative organizations are chaotic and wasteful. In fact, the opposite is true.

They are fine stewards of the company's resources; in fact, when innovation is managed well, the resources come back manyfold to an organization. As Manion (1993, p. 41) points out, "Nursing innovation is the key to transformation of the health care organization and the health care system." By thinking through the five phases of the innovation management process that Manion promotes and by addressing the underlying cultures that can support this five-stage process, nursing organizations will be able to rise above their bureaucratic roots and provide leadership and innovative practices for health care in the future.

Nursing innovation comes not just from the nursing profession. Providing the highest quality of care and service to patients is the passion for many disciplines, and diversity of perceptions is healthy. In the TeamCare redesign experience, the director of the laboratory was the visionary who drove the cultural change at St. Luke's. In the future, innovation will no longer be an option for staff to consider but a requirement if an organization is to stay ahead of its competition.

REFERENCES

Drucker, P. (1985). The discipline of innovation. *Harvard Business Review,* 85(3), 67–72.

Dumaine, B. (1991). Closing the innovation gap. *Fortune, 124*(13), 56–62.

Gleick, J. (1987). *Chaos: Making a new science.* New York: Viking Press.

Harvey, J. (1988). *The Abilene paradox and other meditations on management.* New York: Free Press.

Imai, M. (1986). *Kaizen: The key to Japan's competitive success.* New York: Random House.

Janis, I. (1982). *Groupthink: Psychological studies of policy decision* (2nd ed.). Rapidan, VA: Hartland Publishing.

Japan Human Relations Association Staff (Ed.). (1992). *Kaizen Tein 1: Developing systems for continuous improvement through employee suggestions.* Portland, OR: Productivity Press.

Manion, J. (1993). Chaos of transformation? Managing innovation. *Journal of Nursing Administration, 23*(5), 41–48.

Peters, T. (1992). *Liberation management: Necessary disorganization for the nanosecond nineties.* New York: Knopf.

Quinn, J. (1985). Managing innovation: Controlled chaos. *Harvard Business Review, 85*(3), 73–84.

Shingo, S. (1987). *The sayings of Shigeo Shingo: Key strategies for plant improvement.* Cambridge, MA: Productivity Press.

CHAPTER 3

Cultural Contexts

Culture is the illusive mask that shades our perceptions. It is what Allen and Kraft (1984) called "organizational unconscious"—an unseen giant that represents "those patterns of social behavior and normative expectations that become characteristic of an organization's functioning without its members consciously choosing them" (p. 37).

Within organizations, culture plays a collective role in outlining the norms of conduct for all members. Despite the pervasive nature of culture, experts are not in agreement as to its definition. Schein (1992) believes that organizational culture emerges in response to internal and external environments. Over time, these responses that "worked well enough to be considered valid" (p. 9) become set into cultural patterns. The implication is that changes in culture will occur over time as people interact and find new response patterns that work in new situations.

In Sovie's model (1993), **organizational culture** is defined as shared values and beliefs that affect:

- perceptions of work
- approaches to work
- how people go about work
- organizational interrelatedness

Batey (1992, p. 102) believes culture arises when people share a past, continue to interact frequently, and share a destiny. In this context, culture engulfs a system of beliefs underlying their continuing interactions.

Within the context of redesign, culture is vital but often neglected. Sovie (1993) notes that "hospitals, to survive, must be transformed into responsive organizations capable of new practices that produce improved results" (p. 69).

TABLE 3.1 Core Dimensions of Culture	
DIMENSION	**DESCRIPTION**
Clarity of direction	Formality of planning systems, clear courses of action
Decision making	Level of organization where decisions occur. How systematic are decisions? Is needed information available?
Integration	Coordination, cooperation, and communication among units
Management style	Management deportment, ethics; pattern of encouragement and support to accomplish goals
Ambience	Organizational atmosphere: physical environment, social supports
Performance orientation	Level of accountability for managers and staff
Vitality	Responsiveness to change; pacesetting programs; venturesome goals
Management compensation	Internally equitable, externally competitive, tied to performance; visibility of status symbols and their compatibility with values
Management/employee development	Opportunities for advancement; investment in developmental experiences
Identity	The image projected internally and externally, especially the reputation for quality and fairness
Quality of care	Focus on quality: resources, direction, and support given to quality; how employees judge the quality of the work
Rituals	Rituals to support key goals, values, and cultural principles

Sources: Rowland & Rowland (1992); Del Bueno & Vincent (1994).

CORE DIMENSIONS OF CULTURE

An understanding of the core dimensions of culture will shed light on the complexity of cultural aspects of organizational dynamics. Table 3.1 highlights the core dimensions.

ASSESSING CULTURE

Cultures are shaded from functional (constructive) to dysfunctional (defensive), according to a model by Cooke and Lafferty (1989). Constructive cultures are based on "achievement, self-actualization, encouragement of humanism, and affiliative norms" (McDaniel & Stumpf, 1993, p. 54). These cultures parallel cultures of excellence (Wilson, 1992).

Defensive cultures are seen in two forms. In the passively defensive form, people react in guarded ways due to their need for approval, dependency, and avoidance. Traditional and bureaucratically controlled organizations promote this culture, which resists change and is risk aversive. In the aggressively defensive form, people approach tasks in aggressive ways to protect their status and security (Thomas, Ward, Chorba, & Kumiega, 1990). Competition and perfectionism result in confrontation and power struggles.

Both ends of the spectrum, functional and dysfunctional, are influenced by the strength of the culture. In weak cultures, there is little sense of shared values and expectations. Strong cultures, on the other hand, may be either constructive or defensive.

In order to determine what aspects of hospital culture need to be addressed, the leader must take a serious look at the institution. Table 3.2 compares aspects of culture in functional and dysfunctional organizations, and Figure 3.1 provides a format for assessing functional and dysfunctional aspects of culture in organizations.

ORGANIZATIONAL METAPHORS

Organizations are replete with **metaphors** that transform complex issues into simple images (Del Bueno & Vincent, 1994). Whatever the metaphor, the underlying message is clear. These messages come together to govern part of the culture of each organization. The type of metaphors chosen illustrates relationships and rules of conduct (Table 3.3).

One global metaphor that helps us to understand culture is the term *organizational architecture* (Nadler, Gerstein, & Shaw, 1992). This metaphor, which evokes the concept of building an organization, encompasses more than organizational structure and includes harmony among "constituent design elements" (p. 13) as well as interface with the environment. The concept of moving from a bureaucratic focus to examining the networking facets of the organization enables leaders to develop the linkages necessary for a responsive organization. Four components are essential to this architectural approach (p. 119):

1. information
2. people
3. work
4. technology

Table 3.2 Functional and Dysfunctional Organizational Cultures

Issue	Functional Approach	Dysfunctional Approach
Service	Patient focused, strong	Provider focused, weak
Standards	Clear	Unclear
Decision making	Broad participation	Top down only
		Little staff representation
Employee satisfaction	Actively assessed and improved	Disinterested
Outcomes	Frequent measures	Not measured
	Accountability	No one held accountable
Cost versus Quality	Ongoing assessment	Not measured
	Practices change as result	
	Staff understand costs	Costs unknown to staff
	Cheapest effective approach used	
Education	Systematic, ongoing investment	Education not valued
Teamwork	Strong culture for teams	Stars and turf prominent
	Cooperation across departments	Competition, hoard information
Values	Congruent, shared	Individual, in conflict
	Values equal outcomes	Values do not equal outcomes
Conflict	Dealt with openly and honestly	Submerged

Sources: Sovie (1993); Fleeger (1993).

Table 3.3 Organizational Metaphors

Metaphor	Basis	Symbolism
"It's a battle zone"	Military	Heros
"Chain of command"		Hierarchy
"She's a sacrificial lamb"	Animalistic	Martyr
"Top dog"		Hierarchy
"Well-oiled machine"	Mechanistic	Efficiency
"Mamma Manager"	Social	Maternalism/paternalism
"Team player," "Cheerleader"	Sports	Collective over individual

Figure 3.1 Assessment of an Organizational Culture's Functionality

Functional Approach	Yes	No	Dysfunctional Approach	Yes	No
Service is patient focused, strong.	—	—	Service is provider focused, weak.	—	—
Standards are clear.	—	—	Standards are unclear.	—	—
There is broad participatory decision making.	—	—	There is top-down only decision making.	—	—
			There is little staff representation.	—	—
Administration actively assesses employee satisfaction.	—	—	Administration is disinterested in employee satisfaction.	—	—
Outcomes are frequently measured.	—	—	Outcomes are not measured.	—	—
Appropriate persons are accountable for outcomes.	—	—	People may not be held accountable.	—	—
Ongoing assessment is made of cost versus quality.	—	—	Cost versus quality is not measured.	—	—
Practices change as result.	—	—			
Staff understand costs.	—	—	Costs are unknown to staff.	—	—
Cheapest effective approach is used.	—	—			
There is systematic, ongoing investment in education.	—	—	Education is not valued.	—	—
The culture for teams is strong.	—	—	Stars and turf issues are prominent.	—	—
Cooperation across departments is common.	—	—	Staff are competitive, hoard information.	—	—
Values are congruent, shared.	—	—	Values are individual, in conflict.	—	—
Values equal outcomes.	—	—	Values do not equal outcomes.	—	—
Conflict is dealt with openly and honestly.	—	—	Conflict is submerged.	—	—

Examine the numbers of No answers in the first column and the number of Yes answers in the second column. These are important places to begin changing the organization's culture.

DESIGN PRINCIPLES FOR HIGH-PERFORMANCE WORK SYSTEMS

- **Customer- and environment-focused design**
- **Empowered and autonomous units**
- **Clear direction and goals**
- **Control of variance at the source**
- **Sociotechnical integration**
- **Accessible information flow**
- **Enriched and shared jobs**
- **Empowering human resources practices**
- **Empowering management structure, process, and culture**
- **Capacity to reconfigure (Nadler et al., 1992, pp. 120–123)**

CULTURAL CHANGE

When organizations seek to make major changes, certain cultural conditions support these efforts (Besse, 1957):

- Changes are communicated and understood by employees.
- Security is not threatened.
- People affected by the changes help to create them.
- The changes apply principles of the established culture.
- Changes build on other successful changes.
- Change begins after other changes have been assimilated.
- Changes are well planned.
- New leaders champion the changes.
- People who share the benefits of change support change.
- The organization is accustomed to improvements.

These are important to support on an ongoing basis as a foundation that sets the stage for change. Figure 3.2 provides an assessment format for evaluating cultural readiness for change.

FIGURE 3.2 Cultural Assessment of Support for Change

To what extent are the following statements true on a five-point scale, with 1 = least true and 5 = most true?

1.	Changes are communicated and understood by employees.	1	2	3	4	5
2.	Security is not threatened.	1	2	3	4	5
3.	People affected by the changes help to create them.	1	2	3	4	5
4.	The changes apply principles of established culture.	1	2	3	4	5
5.	Changes build on other successful changes.	1	2	3	4	5
6.	Change begins after other changes have been assimilated.	1	2	3	4	5
7.	Changes are well planned.	1	2	3	4	5
8.	New leaders champion the changes.	1	2	3	4	5
9.	People who share the benefits of change support change.	1	2	3	4	5
10.	The organization is accustomed to improvements.	1	2	3	4	5

Total Score _____

Key: Range 10 – 15 significant resistance to change in culture
         16 – 25 mild resistance to change in culture
         26 – 35 neutral; requires additional support for change
         36 – 45 mild support for change in culture
         46 – 50 optimal culture for supporting change

PRINCIPLES FOR SUCCESSFUL CULTURAL CHANGE

- Be clear about purposes, goals, and tasks.
- Ensure unity of leaders.
- Involve people in the issues that affect them.
- Strive for consensus with a win-win approach.
- Share decision making.
- Focus on results for the short and the long term.
- Integrate concern for people and the bottom line.
- Know your organization and its people.
- Systematically use multilevel change strategies.
- Emphasize sustainable culture changes.
  (Adapted from Allen & Kraft, 1987, p. 28)

These principles indicate good leadership. (The general change theories that apply are covered in detail in Chapter 4.)

ETHICAL LEADERSHIP

Ethical leadership is required for harmony between culture and reality. Leaders have a moral responsibility to uphold the doctrines of the organization (assuming they are morally tenable) and to act consistently. This cannot occur without centeredness: a leader's understanding of the forces that drive him or her, which have been carefully weighed as life philosophies. These undergirding beliefs drive the ethical leader to act in internally consistent ways at all times. It is soothing to an organization to have leaders who act in consistent and predictable ways. People do not have to feel conflict between what they see and what is espoused. Such leaders can truly serve as role models for everyone in the organization and are central to successful redesign.

CREATING CULTURE: STRIVING FOR SYNERGY

People bring to organizations their own cultural contexts, and when these closely held values are in conflict with the organization's norms, problems can arise (Del Bueno & Vincent, 1994). Such personal cultures arise from ethnicity, race, religion, education, social status, and occupation, to name a few.

TIP

One way to bring personal cultures closer to the organizational norm is to show similarities in these beliefs, for example, through visual storyboarding, multidisciplinary presentations, or integrative celebrations that bring together multiple cultural perspectives.

Within health care, for example, there are many professions based on caring principles. "The caring relationship protects the patient from being reduced to the status of an object in the process of treatment of disease or resolution of the problem, hence protecting dignity" (Condon, 1994, p. 46). Caring focuses on the individual rather than taking a generalized approach. Central to a culture that supports a caring environment for clients is one that cares for employees. When these two aspects of caring are in sync, it supports **synergy**; when they are in conflict, it causes dissonance. The effects of such dissonance on the caring environment are not fully understood.

Not every specialty within complex health care organizations comes from the caring arts. The number crunchers and bureaucrats, for example, are far removed from the patient. The challenge for the organization is to help these people see how their actions must be in concert with the culture of caring, the core of health care. Hiring practices should evaluate cultural values of applicants in an effort to attract employees whose personal values are in concert with the organization's.

Martin and Meyerson (1988) identify three types of consistency needed for synergy to occur:

1. **action**
2. **symbols**
3. **content**

In action, content themes are consistent with practices. We walk the walk and talk the talk, as Tom Peters would say. For symbols, congruence is vital between **artifacts**—the rituals and stories that support the myths behind the symbols—and practices. For example, core values that are stated explicitly are expected to be upheld in practice across the organization. Consistency in content means there is congruence among content themes; they do not conflict with one another.

Integration Versus Differentiation

According to Batey (1992), **integration** implies a single culture; **differentiation** recognizes variation across subunits. She carefully points out that differentiation does not necessarily imply conflict but simply variability (p. 109). For example, as redesign progresses throughout an organization, each unit has some unique aspects that evolve due to that unit's culture, patient population needs, and innovation. Other aspects are uniform across all redesign units because of shared principles. The key to success is a balance between consensus and responsiveness to unit needs. Such ambiguity must be acknowledged and accepted as normal.

Sacred Cows and Taboos

Sacred cows are those most revered images of an organization that become the minimum standard of conduct—for example:

- A religiously affiliated organization may require all senior management to be in good standing in the church. This rule is unwritten and unspoken because it is of questionable legality.
- Promptness is expected.
- Thin is in. There are no fat managers.
- There is a myth that must be perpetuated, such as, "We have a mission to the poor and needy" (Del Bueno, 1987, p. 32).

Taboos are similar to sacred cows except that they are sacred must nots. Frequently, taboo ideas are not ever expressed. Some examples of taboos might include:

- Do not ruffle physicians' feathers. You will lose!
- The chain of command must not be abridged.
- Unions are not professional.
- Do not discuss inconsistencies between values and actions.
- Health care workers are protected from layoffs (more socially acceptable might be right sizing).

Organizational Climate Versus Organizational Culture

Organizational climate refers to individual perceptions about the organization; they are thus colored by each person's worldview. When personal culture comes in conflict with organizational culture, the climate will be seen as negative (Marquis & Huston, 1992). There may be wide variability in how individuals view the organization's climate. In contrast, organizational culture refers to the collective beliefs held by the majority in the organization. The stronger the culture of an organization is, the more tightly held are those collective beliefs.

One factor that is thought to influence the strength of an organization's culture is the reliance on part-time employees, who often have limited orientation or ongoing exposure to the institutional norms. Of particular concern is the trend to hire temporary workers, who enjoy no benefits or organizational status. Especially in the case of "**knowledge workers**," it is important to secure commitment and buy-in to resolve organizational issues. What effects do issues such as weekend-only staff and off-shifts have on organizational culture, and how can that culture be better extended to these workers?

NETWORKS FOR CHANGE

The importance of communication networks to the acceptance of change is clear. Timing, tone, and inclusiveness help to relieve fears of the unknown and boost support for change. Bungled communication efforts magnify distrust and grandstanding by individuals who feel at risk. In addition to communication networks, leaders have at their disposal other important tools to revamp culture in support of redesign efforts. Their skillful use of these tools can ensure success.

TOOLS FOR REDESIGNING CULTURE

- **Establish new assumptions that are made explicit.**
  Example: The patient is the focus of the institution, and all operations must center on the patient.
- **Create new stories, myths, and rituals that reflect the desired culture.**
  Example: Establish walking, bedside report that includes the patient/family in planning care.
- **Change the physical environment to support the new culture.**
  Example: Eliminate central nurses' stations and create satellite stations to encourage patient-focused care.
- **Challenge sacred cows.**
  Example: Examine the need for compartmentalized departments.

- **Change the structure to facilitate new goals.**
  Example: If shared decision making is desired, invest the nursing shared governance structure with the same authority as the medical council.
- **Target reward systems to the new goals.**
  Example: Pay unit staff for performance against standards for quality, efficiency, and outcome.
- **Eliminate barriers that paralyze action.**
  Example: Establish task forces that cross departmental barriers, and give them authority to solve problems.
- **Examine systems to ensure they support goals.**
  Example: Determine whether the computer system gives vital information.
- **Enlist new employees, and train them for redesign.**
  Example: Orientation with supportive preceptors helps new employees fit in with desired norms without having to unlearn old behaviors.
- **Educate and coach for success.**
  Example: Identify key skills and attitudes needed for success, and then target education with an outcome focus. Value education.

POLITICAL REALITIES

There are political realities that affect each organization's culture, particularly sacred cows and taboos. Leaders must carefully assess the political dynamics and pick their battles to achieve the maximum benefit within an acceptable level of risk.

The cumulative effect of change on the organization also must be considered. In these turbulent times, managing change within the confines of what the organization can tolerate is a very important task. That necessitates a clear understanding of priorities.

TIP

Education is crucial for successful change. Educators usually have great expert power within the organization. They can model new behaviors needed in redesign—or perpetuate the status quo. Strategies that enlist key educators to facilitate change are vital. Educational materials and curricula should be evaluated for consistency with change objectives.

One dynamic that redesign affects is roles. Roles are an essential element of culture—a sacred cow of a sorts. Introducing new categories of caregivers upsets that dynamics, and confusion about priorities, job boundaries, delegation skills, and expanded accountabilities must be discussed and resolved. Staff must be involved in decisions that affect their practice because those changes cannot be dictated by a third party with no clinical credibility. A retreat to assist staff in evaluating new roles in patient-focused care can be a valuable experience (Figure 3.3).

Another approach that is helpful in clarifying roles with staff is to discuss the state's nurse practice act. Each state's act discusses delegation by RNs to assistive personnel and outlines the responsibilities that accompany delegation. Many have wording that refers to the RN's being the only nursing level allowed to make decisions requiring "simultaneous judgment." This act of simultaneous judgment is the illusive nature of professional nursing that often gets lost in a task-oriented approach to care.

Nurses deserve a delivery system that supports professional nursing practice. More important, patients and their loved ones deserve the highest-quality care possible. The journey to changing the way a unit practices is not one others can map out for the unit. Each unit as a group must decide its standards and set its assignment patterns apart from history and convention. Here are some thoughts on professional nursing practice to use with staff nurses to help in defining roles.

THOUGHTS ON PROFESSIONAL NURSING PRACTICE

- **Describe the RN, LPN, and technician roles. Have you identified only tasks? Is that how you want to define your practice?**
- **Describe what is unique to the RN role. Are you able to fulfill these unique responsibilities using your current assignment and delivery system? Which ones get left to the end of a busy day or are not accomplished at all? Can you articulate these roles clearly to others on your team so that they can value supporting your effort to achieve that level of practice?**
- **Describe a situation from your practice that you recall gave you the greatest joy in nursing. Does your current practice focus on the kinds of roles that your example illustrates?**
- **How often do you go home feeling you have truly connected with your patients in a meaningful way? Is the joy still there in your**

FIGURE 3.3 Patient-Focused-Care Retreat

Objectives

1. Define the principles that will guide the design of patient-focused care.

2. Clarify roles needed for patient-focused care and how these roles must interact.

3. Analyze the delivery system needed to provide professional patient-focused care.

4. Develop a plan to move forward with the design of patient-focused care.

Agenda

I. Introduction/vision for the retreat

II. "Perfect Work World" exercise, on a flip chart (done from a patient-centered perspective)

    A. List the care given that is most meaningful to patients.

    B. List the characteristics of a perfect work world and values that drive that vision of that perfect world.

III. Principles of patient-focused care

    A. Identify guiding principles of patient-focused care.

    B. What current practices do not fulfill these principles?

IV. What is professional practice?

    A. Define legal basis of practice.

    B. Identify scope of RN, LPN, and technician roles.

    C. Leave old baggage at the door.

V. Role clarification for professional practice

    A. Distinguish RN roles that are vital to professional practice.

    B. How satisfied are we with the way we currently meet these requirements?

    C. Describe how LPNs and technicians can support professional care activities/patient care needs.

VI. Delivery system

    A. Given the scope of roles, patient-focused principles, and coordinated care needs, analyze how teams might function to accomplish patient goals.

    B. How would a typical day's assignments for a team look in this model?

    C. What skills do team members need to allow this level of practice to thrive?

VII. Implementation planning

    A. Design a team/assignment model for professional practice.

    B. What are the priorities? Assume a six-month time line.

    C. Who should be involved in the planning?

    D. Ask for volunteers for leadership roles.

service to others? What about your work environment supports that happening frequently? What prevents it from occurring?

- Does every patient on your floor have care that is directed by an RN? That is, does an RN assess needs, make judgments as to the plan of care, and delegate based on nursing judgment in every instance requiring simultaneous judgment?
- Do you as the RN view yourself as accountable for every patient on the team, or have you abdicated your legal duty to others? (Do you mentally refer to the "LPN's patients" and not fully attend to their needs that only you are qualified to fulfill? I am not talking about tasks!)
- Are you as the RN focusing on tasks or functioning at a higher level that focuses on your responsibility to coordinate care?
- Identify the principles of practice that you want to embrace for your units. Design your assignments to support these principles. Equity does not mean everyone has the same assignment. Assignments should be made after considering breadth and depth of responsibility and focus of each job.

Teamwork and collaboration will be the hallmarks of successful change. Change masters realign resources in pursuit of goals. Some people will choose not to become players; they will be left behind. There are political implications to how an organization's culture deals with nonplayers. These people have to be dealt with in a way consistent with the culture.

SUMMARY

Culture plays a pivotal role in the success of every organization. Core dimensions of culture, ways to assess culture, and techniques for cultural change were addressed in this chapter within the framework of ethical leadership and political realities. Leaders who do not address culture fool themselves when they attempt to enact change using only operational and structural concepts. Aligning with your organization's cultural needs also will crystalize into better leadership and vision for future directions.

REFERENCES

Allen, R. F., & Kraft, C. (1987). *The organizational unconscious: How to create the corporate culture you want and need.* Morristown, NJ: Human Resource Institute.

Allen, R. F., & Kraft, C. (1984). Transformations that last: A cultural approach. In J. D. Adams (Ed.), *Transforming work* . Alexandria, VA: Miles River Press.

Batey, M. V. (1992). Organizational culture: Analysis of the concept. In P. J. Decker & E. J. Sullivan (Eds.), *Nursing administration: A micro/macro approach for effective nurse executives* (pp. 101–111). Norwalk, CT: Appleton & Lange.

Besse, R. (1957). Company planning must be planned. *Dun's Review and Modern Industry, 69*(4), 62–63.

Condon, E. H. (1994). Nursing and the caring metaphor: Gender and political influences on an ethics of care. In E. C. Hein & M. J. Nicholson (Eds.), *Contemporary leadership behavior: Selected readings.* Philadelphia: Lippincott.

Cooke, R. A., & Lafferty, J. C. (1989). *Organizational culture inventory.* Plymouth, MI: Human Synergistics.

Del Bueno, D. J. (1987). An organizational checklist. *Journal of Nursing Administration, 17*(5), 30–33.

Del Bueno, D. J., & Vincent, P. M. (1994). Organizational culture. How important is it? In E. C. Hein & M. J. Nicholson (Eds.), *Contemporary leadership behavior: Selected readings.* Philadelphia: Lippincott.

Fleeger, M. E. (1993). Assessing organizational culture: A planning strategy. *Nursing Management, 24*(2), 39–41.

Marquis, B. L., & Huston, C. J. (1992). *Leadership roles and management functions in nursing.* Philadelphia: Lippincott.

Martin, J., & Meyerson, D. (1988). Organizational culture and the denial, channeling and acknowledgement of ambiguity. In L. R. Pondy, R. J. Boland, & N. Thomas (Eds.), *Managing ambiguity and change* (pp. 93–125). New York: Wiley.

McDaniel, C., & Stumpf, L. (1993). The organizational culture: Implications for nursing service. *Journal of Nursing Administration, 23*(4), 54–60.

Nadler, D. A., Gerstein, M. S., Shaw, R. B. & Associates. (1992). *Organizational architecture: Designs for changing organizations.* San Francisco: Jossey-Bass.

Rowland, H. S., & Rowland, B. L. (1992). *Nursing administration handbook (3rd ed.).* Gaithersburg, MD: Aspen.

Schein, E. H. (1992). *Organizational culture and leadership (2nd Ed.).* San Francisco: Jossey-Bass.

Schiemann, W. A. (1992). Why change fails. *Across the Board, 29*(4), 53–54.

Sovie, M. D. (1993). Hospital culture—Why create one? *Nursing Economics, 11*(2), 69–75.

Thomas, C., Ward, M., Chorba, C., Kumiega, A. (1990). Measuring and interpreting organizational culture. *Journal of Nursing Administration, 20*(6), 17–24.

Wilson, C. K. (1992). *Building new nursing organizations: Visions and realities.* Gaithersburg, MD: Aspen.

CHAPTER 4

Dynamics of Change

GAIL L. INGERSOLL

That organizations change is certain. That individuals within organizations embrace change is not. A multitude of personal, environmental, and institutional characteristics interact to facilitate or hinder organizational change. In this chapter, issues associated with planned and unplanned change and recommendations for improving the potential for successful outcome are described.

DRIVING FORCES

Economics is often the driving force behind organizational change. External demands or internal financial constraints prompt organizations to reexamine how they manage their business. These driving forces may evolve slowly over the course of several years or may erupt quickly as a result of legislative mandates or the need for immediate response to new competitive markets. Recently, experts have begun challenging this reactor model of change and have stressed the value of an entrepreneurial approach in which creativity and vision are the guiding principles behind selection of alternatives.

In these environments, managers facilitate the work of the group, foster creativity, and challenge workers to try out new ideas and approaches to problem solving.

TIP

Today, successful health care agencies are those that nourish a climate of continuous change (Sherman, 1993).

SYSTEMATIC CHANGE AS A FOUNDATION FOR REDESIGN

Three types of change have been described (Kaluzny & Hernandez, 1988): **technical change**, which involves modifications of the organization's usual activities but not adjustment of the goals of the institution; **transitional change**, which alters the goals but not how they are achieved; and **transformational change**, which includes both the organization's goals and the means for achieving them. Transformational change is the most dramatic form; it requires creation of new paradigms and produces the most disruption. Consequently, it is the least common. (See Table 4.1.)

Hospital care delivery systems changes, write Dienemann and Gessner (1992), can be either **job design focused** or, less frequently, **systems redesign focused**. These authors define job design restructuring processes as bottom-up approaches in which the division of labor is restructured within the nursing unit to improve productivity and job satisfaction. They believe these designs have little impact on the organization's structure and are unlikely to produce significant effect since influential care providers within the organization are not involved. Systems redesigns, on the other hand, use a top-down approach and focus on the interdependence of multiple groups or departments in which competing goals are likely. Examples are **total quality management** (TQM) programs and **patient-focused care delivery** (PFC) models. These approaches are expected to produce more dramatic, long-lasting effects since multiple stakeholders are included in the change process and the focus is on patient care delivery rather than the workers.

Because few studies of top-down versus bottom-up approaches have been conducted, Dienemann and Gessner's statements should be interpreted with caution. Studies by Ingersoll et al. (Ingersoll, Ryan, & Schultz, 1990; Ingersoll, Schultz, Ryan, & Kitzman, 1993), Verran et al. (Gerber, Verran, & Milton, 1993; Milton, Verran, Murdaugh, & Gerber, 1992) and Weisman et al.

TABLE 4.1 Types of Change

TYPE	FOCUS OF CHANGE	IMPACT ON ORGANIZATION
Technical	Individual activities	Limited
Transitional	Goals	Limited to partial
Transformational	Goals; processes for achieving goals	Significant

(Gordon, Weisman, Bergner, Wong, & Cassard, 1993; Weisman, Gordon, Cassard, Bergner, & Wong, 1993) suggest that unit-focused approaches are quite useful for initiating change. Their studies of professional practice models found that as long as central administration is supportive, a bottom-up approach is an effective method for initiating change. Moreover, participants in a unit-focused approach are likely to be more fully informed and remain committed to the change since its impact is felt immediately and the changes directly affect their work environment. Simply exposing greater numbers of individuals to an innovation does not guarantee the change will proceed as intended.

The change process is a complex one, and experts now are breaking it down into more precise stages than the simple "freezing," "unfreezing," and "refreezing" framework used in the past. Perlman and Takacs (1990) have identified ten phases of organizational change, each of which is recognized by distinctive characteristics and each of which requires specific management skills to keep the change process moving (Table 4.2).

Throughout the change process, managers must recognize how potentially disruptive the event will be. Ongoing support and opportunities to grieve the loss of the old ways are necessary. In addition, information about the change, the rationale for it, and its expected outcome should be provided early and consistently throughout the process. The manager must never assume that once information is given, the process can proceed with only brief updates when something is added. Multiple opportunities for explanation and discussion about how the change will affect individuals should be provided. Moreover, different ways of delivering the information should be used—for example, group information sessions, individual counseling, and written memos and documents.

BARRIERS AND FACILITATORS

Characteristics of the organization contribute either positively or negatively to change. Recognizing and removing or reducing barriers and maximizing facilitators increases the likelihood for successful outcome. Rarely, if ever, is the manager able to remove all barriers, and in fact, this may not be desirable. Barriers within the organization force people to think more creatively about how to overcome them. In addition, barriers (whether people or resources) challenge the change makers to clarify and refine the goals for change to ensure the change is worth the effort needed to overcome the barriers.

TABLE 4.2 Ten Stages Of Organizational Change

STAGE	COMMON CHARACTERISTICS	MANAGEMENT STRATEGIES
1. Equilibrium	Feelings of well-being High energy	Provide early information about the intended change and what to anticipate Continue with information
2. Denial	Withdrawal from new ideas Persistent behaviors to reinforce existing work environment	Provide support and offer opportunities to grieve loss while reinforcing the need for the change Recognize and support the perceived loss
3. Anger	Acting-out behaviors Blaming Negative comments directed toward management and others perceived as responsible for the change	Assist individuals with developing positive problem-solving strategies and effective techniques for dealing with anger
4. Bargaining	Attempts to modify change so it fits into what already exists Refusal to admit change will occur according to original plans	Consider recommendations that may be appropriate and may increase the chances for successful implementation of change. Reinforce the intent to continue with change Seek input from multiple stakeholders Ensure bargaining activities do not stall progress
5. Chaos	Feelings of powerlessness Turnover may occur because of feelings of frustration	Continue with opportunities for expression of concerns Realize increased structure may be necessary Provide clear indication of direction
6. Depression	Expression of feelings of sorrow Withdrawal and reduced productivity	Offer support (formal mechanisms for dealing with loss may be required)
7. Resignation	Giving up of the old with reluctant acceptance of the new Wistful comments about "what used to be"	Provide direction Look for ways to demonstrate early positive outcomes of change Continue to clarify the components of the change
8. Openness	Increased energy level Increased receptivity to information Attempts to make the change personally meaningful	Reexplain the change components Provide positive reinforcement as behaviors improve
9. Readiness	Creative thinking in relation to the new	Provide positive reinforcement of creative ideas Clarify mechanisms for problem solving associated with change
10. Reemergence	Feelings of ownership of the new New ideas generated High productivity resumes	Continue with refinement of change: use new energy to move process along more quickly Clarify responsibilities for maintaining change

Source: From the 10 STAGES OF CHANGE by Dottie Perlman and George J.Takacs, adapted and reprinted with permission from *Nursing Management*, (Vol 21, No 4, April 1990).

Barriers

Some barriers to change involve the following:

- *Organizational inertia.* Slow-moving organizations tend to remain slow moving unless something (or someone) forces them along.
- *Organizational history.* "The way we've always done things" stifles idea generation and creativity. Old ways are held sacred primarily because they produce a sense of comfort and familiarity. New approaches threaten existing power structures and create uncertainty.
- *Laws of the land.* Over time, "the way we've always done things" also tends to become common practice. Because these laws of practice are part of the organization's culture and have significance to its members, individuals who attempt to challenge or change them may be ostracized by the group.
- *Bargain basement shopping.* Because of financial constraints and the need to cut costs immediately, administrators who are given a range of choices may select the ones that appear to be the cheapest. The focus on immediate cost reductions prompts quick solutions in which dollars are saved immediately, but these options often prove to be less desirable over time.
- *Communication breakdown.* Inefficient or sporadic communication within the organization slows and disrupts change. Conflicting information contributes to breakdown; when management sends one message one moment and another the next, employees waste a significant amount of time trying to figure out which message is the real one.
- *Bureaucratic red tape.* Layers of inefficiency dishearten even the most enthusiastic employees. Flat organizations are more likely to respond quickly to innovations and to keep information moving freely back and forth.
- *Mission impossible.* If the vision for the organization is untenable or too divergent from what currently exists, significant resistance is likely. Although the vision may be reasonable based on the administrator's understanding of the future, without appreciation for the difficulties associated with giving up existing ideals or the need to build the vision on top of what exists, the potential for failure is great.
- *Poor fit between the organization's values and actions.* When the organization's actions differ from its stated values or from the values of its associates, confusion and chaos result. If the change is the result of a shift in values, members of the organization need to be informed about why the change in values is occurring. In health care organizations in which cost constraints produce changes in service delivery, this

often results in expressed concerns about the sacrifice of the goal of quality care. Reductions and changes are perceived to be inconsistent with the organization's values.

- *Employee segregation.* When employees in organizations work only among themselves and are rarely exposed to other subgroups within the organization, resistance to new ideas or approaches from "outsiders" may occur. The more that individuals interact with others from outside their usual work groups, the more likely they are to develop a global vision of the organization.

- *Sensory overload.* When multiple significant changes occur at once or immediately following one another, associates begin showing signs of sensory overload. They long for a break so they can recover. In many cases they are willing to continue with the change process, but they want some time to regroup and recover before proceeding. This problem is particularly acute today when multiple dramatic changes are occurring simultaneously within health care organizations. Associates have little time to adjust to one major change when they are asked to prepare for another.

- *Fear of failure.* Creative people need freedom to create. When they fear their creative mistakes will result in punishment, demotion, or ridicule, they opt for the safe choice and shelve the creative ideas they perceive to be too risky.

- *Complexity.* The greater the number of components associated with any change, the more likely it is to fail (Shortell, Morrison, & Friedman, 1992). When complex changes are introduced, managers should work to break the process into manageable pieces, ones in which some evidence of positive effect can be seen early.

- *Diversity.* When the components of a change are interrelated and dependent on one another, it is more difficult to separate them into manageable units. As a result, the change is at greater risk of failure (Shortell, Morrison, & Friedman, 1992).

Facilitators

Facilitators to change help negate or minimize the effect of barriers and include the following:

- *Managerial self-reflection.* The ability of managers to analyze and understand how their behaviors contribute to organizational inertia and disruption enhances the potential for positive change (Morgan, 1989).

- *Managerial visibility and accessibility.* Many well-meaning managers fail by handing off responsibility and then disappearing from view. In an attempt to demonstrate confidence in the group's ability to carry the work forward, the manager mistakenly underestimates the group process and decision-making skills required before group members can work together effectively. Group members with little to no experience in group decision-making processes flounder and are frustrated by a sense of powerlessness and failure. Clear descriptions of boundaries for decision making and the final approval process also need to be specified at the outset. Otherwise tension will occur if groups proceed believing they have final decision-making authority when in fact the decision is to be made by someone else.

- *Teams of individuals.* Decision making and idea generation are enhanced by teams whose members work both individually and collectively to foster change. When the focus of members is solely on the team, constant compromise and mediocrity result. When members work consistently toward consensus, spontaneous or outrageous ideas may be withheld for fear of disrupting or slowing the work of the group. On the other hand, if individuals within the team perceive that their success in the institution is based on beating out everyone else, dysfunctional rivalry may result.

- *Freedom to act.* When individuals are encouraged to think creatively and to solve problems, they do so. In successful organizations, employees are given problems to solve rather than solutions to questions (Kanter, 1983).

- *Tolerance for ambiguity.* Successful organizations are those in which ambiguity is part of the daily work environment (Kanter, 1983). This ambiguity allows things to happen. People generate ideas to reduce the tension and are given time to try out solutions, realizing that some rough spots are likely in the early stages of change.

- *Commitment to development of associates.* When organizations demonstrate a commitment to associates' development needs, associates respond with commitment to the organization. When associates are effectively prepared for change, resistance and false starts are reduced.

- *Program divisibility.* When new programs can be subdivided into manageable components, the process associated with initiating the change seems less formidable (Shortell, Morrison, & Friedman, 1992).

- *Program reversibility.* When the proposed change, or its subcomponents, can be deleted if they prove to be problematic, less resistance to their initiation is likely (Shortell, Morrison, & Friedman, 1992). This facilitator can itself become a barrier, however, if managers resist making major revisions for fear of their irreversibility. Managers may opt to introduce small, ineffective measures that tend to stall change and maintain the status quo.

- *Wiggle room.* When organizations are rigid and job descriptions are defined too precisely, little room for flexibility and shifting of responsibility is possible. Organizations with loosely defined job descriptions and guidelines rather than rules for behavior are more likely to be successful in shifting activities from one associate to another and in responding quickly to recommended change. When redesign efforts are attempted in organizations with rigid boundaries, the resultant change is often small and insignificant (Oldham & Hackman, 1980).

Assessing Organizational Readiness

Before initiating any major organizational change, an assessment of organizational readiness is ideal. This concept, a fairly new one, incorporates information from previous descriptions of organizations that have been successful at initiating and sustaining change. Sherman (1993) acknowledges this need in his three-stage sequencing plan for initiating organizational change:

1. preparation
2. implementation
3. acceleration

In the first stage, preparation, assessment of organizational readiness is identified. Implementation and acceleration, the second and third stages, take approximately two years to complete.

A principal outcome of organizational readiness assessment is a plan for the timing of the change. If an innovation is introduced when the level of organizational readiness is low, negative response or delayed acceptance is likely. The effective manager may need to complete preparatory work prior to initiating the change. In this way, readiness increases, along with the potential for successful outcome.

A useful component of a readiness assessment is a description of the organization's culture and whether subgroup cultures within the organization are consistent with the organization's. When disparity between the subgroup and the organization is present, conflict and resistance are likely. In addition, Kilmann (1988) describes the negative influence of what he calls "culture rut" on change. When members of the organization are in a culture rut, they behave without questioning. Repeated actions produce no results, and pressures from within the work group support the status quo, keeping members from breaking out of the cycle. Morale and performance suffer. Breaking the culture rut requires consistent attention to the desired vision and specific strategies for moving in that direction. It also may entail removing individuals who are unable to envision the organization in any other way.

ORGANIZATIONAL CULTURE

Organizational culture is defined as a system of shared meanings and a pattern of beliefs, values, expectations, and behaviors that characterize the organization (Deresky, cited by Chelte, Hess, Fanelli, & Ferris, 1989). Organizational culture is developed and shaped by the ongoing interaction of the members of the organization and by the choices they make (Brannen, 1991). It is not always easy to recognize, particularly if different subcultures within the organization blur the picture. Subcultures develop because of the tendency of organizations to assign individuals to groups based on job level or function (Cooke & Rousseau, 1988), where similar commitment and experiences reinforce the norms. Individuals who fail to adapt to the culture usually leave because of the stress between their own values and beliefs and those of the dominant group.

Cooke and Rousseau (1988) describe two attributes of culture: *direction,* which involves the content or substance of the culture, demonstrated through the members' behaviors, and *intensity*, the strength of the content or substance of the culture. Intensity is an outcome of the degree of consensus among group members and the potential for the group's behaviors to obtain meaningful rewards. As Sovie (1993) notes, changing organizational culture is not easy and may require bringing in a new leadership team from the outside. New leaders often are more willing to confront problems in the existing environment and can create the momentum needed to make substantial change. To do so, an organizational assessment and thorough understanding of the culture is needed. Some helpful strategies for identifying and describing organizational culture are listed in Figure 4.1.

FIGURE 4.1 Strategies for Identifying Organizational Culture

- Observe the physical layout of the organization. Is it purely functional? Or is there evidence of the valuing of individuality and personal space? Pay attention to what is missing, also (Ott, 1989). For example, do administrators speak about their commitment to group decision making and yet there is no conference room or space where more than 2 to 3 individuals can meet?

- Review documents about the organization; look for discrepancies between what is written and what is observed or heard. Compare official documents distributed to the public to those prepared for internal use only.

- Review meeting minutes and other records of events.

- Interview individuals at all levels of the organization.

- Listen to words/phrases used by associates to describe the organization.

- Ask associates to describe the values of the organization.

- Observe interactions between associates, between associates and consumers, and between associates and management.

- Determine reporting relationships and decision-making processes.

- Conduct focus groups in which participants talk about their values and their beliefs about and expectations for the organization. Ask them to relate stories and myths about the organization and to talk about the ways in which associates are recognized for their contributions.

- Use organizational assessment questionnaires.

The assessment of organizational culture usually uncovers potential barriers and facilitators to change. It also gives clues to the organization's readiness, which may be recognized by the characteristics shown in Figure 4.2.

Organizational culture, organizational readiness and a third factor, organizational commitment, may influence both the likelihood of change occurring and the overall extent of the outcome of the change. Organizations with cultures that are internally consistent and directed toward a common goal are more likely to embrace change and to work toward attainment of that goal. Organizations with a high level of readiness for change are more likely to move the change along quickly and successfully. In addition, organizations in which associates are committed to the success of the organization are more likely to experience smoother transitions and steadier progress toward the outcome. The potential for successful outcome is maximized when all three contributors are favorable.

An examination of barriers and facilitators presented earlier reveals that many of these are associated with organizational culture, organizational commitment, or organizational readiness. Barriers and facilitators associated with organizational culture include:

- organizational culture
- organizational history
- fit between the organization's values and actions
- employee segregation
- fear of failure
- managerial self-reflection
- managerial visibility and accessibility
- teams of individuals
- freedom to act
- tolerance for ambiguity
- commitment to associate development
- wiggle room

Those associated with organizational commitment include:

- employee segregation
- managerial visibility and accessibility
- teams of individuals
- freedom to act
- commitment to associate development

FIGURE 4.2 Clues to Organizational Readiness

- Existence of jobs with high levels of autonomy, skill variety, task identity (degree to which job requires completion of an identifiable piece of work), and feedback (information about how associates are performing) (Hackman & Oldham, 1976; Oldham & Hackman, 1980).
- Associates who perceive their contributions to the organization are directly related to outcomes.
- History of positive outcomes associated with change.
- Committed, enthusiastic leaders with a clear vision for the future.
- Consistency between the organization's subcultures and the overall culture of the organization.
- Associates who are committed to the organization (Steers, 1977).
- Collaborative relationships among associates; managers who participate in and support collaboration at all levels.
- Effective, speedy communication systems in place.
- History of attention to organizational and management practices.
- History of multiple strategies to manage cultural and organizational issues.

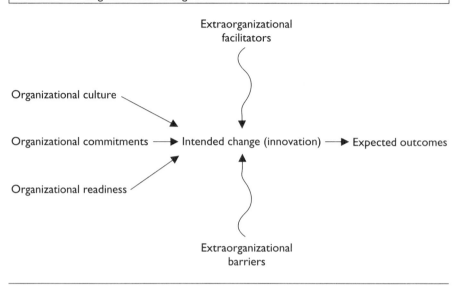

FIGURE 4.3 Organizational Change Model

Level of organizational readiness is affected by each of the barriers and facilitators included previously. Assumedly, each barrier or facilitator contributes to whether the organization will be ready to accept and follow through with the changes proposed.

Additional barriers and facilitators exist external to the organization (Figure 4.3). Extraorganizational barriers and facilitators might include the state of the economy, local and state legislative constraints, the number and proximity of market competitors, and the availability of community resources to support the proposed changes.

NEGOTIATING THE VISION

One of the most promising approaches for negotiating a vision for change involves intrainstitutional and interinstitutional collaboration (Morgan, 1989). Collaboration within and across organizations maximizes the potential for creative idea generation. It does add to the complexity of the change process, however, since additional people are involved and multiple viewpoints are offered. Nonetheless, the likelihood of improved outcome is increased when individuals with diverse ideas and perspectives work toward a common goal.

Whether organizational redesign occurs depends on the strengths of the administrative group and its ability to transform associates. No single administrator can accomplish the changes needed in health care organizations today; rather, both administrators and associates must make a concerted effort.

Essential characteristics and vision begin with the chief executive officers of the organization. They need sufficient energy and stamina to keep things moving even in the most turbulent of times. Organizational redesign takes a significant amount of time, and no administrator should underestimate the skill and savvy required of those who are able to do it. As Sherman (1993) notes, in the early stages of redesign, the energy and drive come from the senior executive group. If those individuals do not have a clear vision for the change or the commitment to the work, the project is certain to fail.

Successful administrators also establish formal and informal mechanisms to keep the organization flooded with information. They work to ensure that stakeholders (anyone likely to be affected by the change) are given as much information as possible as soon as possible. Visibility and approachability are essential throughout the process to ensure that everyone involved in the redesign is able to provide input and ask questions. Well-intentioned administrators often start the change process by holding frequent information sessions designed to get everyone geared up but then disappear into their offices as the change process begins to drag on.

Participants in organizational redesign have difficulty seeing evidence of movement because they are focused on the day-to-day work of making the change happen. Using benchmarks and designing a formal process evaluation strategy help participants visualize the process and the extent of the change. One such approach was used successfully during the introduction of an enhanced professional practice model for nurses. Using this approach, staff nurses and administrators were successful in moving the involved patient care unit from a global perspective of the desired vision for change to a specific strategy for ensuring that it happened (Ingersoll, Bazar, & Zentner, 1993).

TIP

During the change process, efforts should be made to identify specific benchmarks that provide evidence of change. These benchmarks help keep the change process on target and provide a tangible indication of the movement that is occurring as a result of the changes.

Throughout the process, decision making should occur at the lowest possible level (Sherman, 1993). Barriers to this process and existing approval mechanisms that limit or prevent it from happening should be removed. Most barriers to decision making have been introduced to protect organizations from the mistakes of its associates. In redesigned organizations where risk taking and some mistakes are expected, these control mechanisms are no longer needed.

SUMMARY

Change is an essential component of any living organization. Successful health care agencies of the future will be those in which change is an everyday occurrence. Organizations that welcome change as an opportunity to create will survive; those that do not will not. In this chapter, barriers and facilitators to change and strategies for making it happen have been identified.

REFERENCES

Brannen, M. Y. (1991). Culture as the critical factor in implementing innovation. *Business Horizons, 34*(6), 59–67.

Chelte, A. F., Hess, P., Fanelli, R., & Ferris, W. P. (1989). Corporate culture as an impediment to employee involvement. When you can't get there from here. *Work and Occupations, 16,* 153–164.

Cooke, R. A., & Rousseau, D. M. (1988). Behavioral norms and expectations. A quantitative approach to the assessment of organizational culture. *Groups and Organization Studies, 13,* 245–273.

Dienemann, J., & Gessner, T. (1992). Restructuring nursing care delivery systems. *Nursing Economics, 10,* 253–258.

Gerber, R., Verran, J., & Milton, D. (1993, November). Differentiated group professional practice: Research model testing. In P. Moritz (Chair), *Innovative nursing practice models: Common issues and implications.* Symposium conducted at the ANA Council of Nurse Researchers Scientific Session, Washington, DC.

Gordon, D. L., Weisman, C., Bergner, M., Wong, R., & Cassard, S. (1993, November). Unit model for reorganizing hospital nursing resources. In P. Moritz (Chair), *Innovative nursing practice models: Common issues and implications.* Symposium conducted at the ANA Council of Nurse Researchers Scientific Session, Washington, DC.

Hackman, J. R., & Oldham, G. R. (1976). Motivation through the design to work: Test of a theory. *Organizational Behavior and Human Performance, 16,* 250–279.

Ingersoll, G. L., Bazar, M. T., & Zentner, J. B. (1993). Monitoring unit-based innovations: A process evaluation approach. *Nursing Economics, 11,* 137–143.

Ingersoll, G. L., Ryan, S. A., & Schultz, A. W. (1990). Evaluating the impact of enhanced professional practice on patient outcome. In I. E. Gertzen (Ed.), *Differentiating nursing practice: Into the twenty-first century* (pp. 301–313). Kansas City, MO: American Academy of Nursing.

Ingersoll, G. L., Schultz, A. W., Ryan, S. A., & Hitzman, H. (1993, November). Effect of enhanced professional practice on patient outcome. In P. Moritz (Chair), *Innovative nursing practice models: Common issues and implications.* Symposium conducted at the ANA Council of Nurse Researchers Scientific Session, Washington, DC.

Kaluzny, A. D., & Hernandez, S. R. (1988). Organizational change and innovation. In S. M. Shortell & A. D. Kaluzny (Eds.), *Healthcare management: A text in organization theory and behavior* (2nd ed.). Albany, NY: Delmar Publishers, Inc.

Kanter, R. M. (1983). *The change masters.* New York: Simon & Schuster.

Kilmann, R. H. (1988). Management of corporate culture. In M. D. Fottler, R. Hernandez, & C. L. Joiner (Eds.), *Strategic management of human resources in health services organizations.* Albany, NY: Delmar Publishers, Inc.

Kimberly, J. R., & Quinn, R. E. (1984). *Managing organizational transitions.* Homewood, IL: Richard D. Irwin.

Milton, D., Verran, J., Murdaugh, C., & Gerber, R. (1992). Differentiated group professional practice in nursing: A demonstration model. *Nursing Clinics of North America, 27,* 23–30.

Morgan, G. (1989). *Creative organization theory: A sourcebook.* Newbury Park, CA: Sage Publications.

Morgan, G. (1986). *Images of organization.* Newbury Park, CA: Sage Publications.

Oldham, G. R., & Hackman, J. R. (1980). Work design in the organizational context. In B. M. Staw & L. L. Cummings (Eds.), *Research in organizational behavior* (vol. 2, pp. 247–278). Greenwich, CT: JAI Press.

Ott, J. S. (1989). *The organizational culture perspective.* Chicago: Dorsey Press.

Perlman, D., & Takacs, G. J. (1990). The 10 stages of change. *Nursing Management, 21*(4), 33–38.

Sherman, V. C. (1993). *Creating the new American hospital.* San Francisco: Jossey-Bass.

Shortell, S. M., Morrison, E. M., & Friedman, B. (1992). *Strategic choices for America's hospitals: Managing change in turbulent times.* San Francisco: Jossey-Bass.

Sovie, M. D. (1993). Hospital culture—why create one? *Nursing Economics, 11,* 69–75.

Steers, R. M. (1977). Antecedents and outcomes of organizational commitment. *Administrative Science Quarterly, 22,* 46–56.

Weisman, C. S., Gordon, D. L., Cassard, S. D., Bergner, M., & Wong, R. (1993). The effects of unit self-management on hospital nurses' work process, work satisfaction, and retention. *Medical Care, 31,* 381–393.

CHAPTER 5

Analyzing Work Flow:

The Key to Continuous Improvement

KATHRYN J. PARKS

Long ago a story was told about a rabbi who was challenged by a student. "Why do you always answer a question with a question?" queried the student. "There's something wrong with questions?" retorted the rabbi.

Most tools of quality improvement and redesign involve critically examining current practice—an exercise that almost automatically moves you toward redesign and change. Hofmann's sequential steps for critical path development (Focus Phase, Analyze Phase, Develop Phase, Execute Phase) and other critical path development tools inherently involve asking questions (Figure 5.1). Analyzing work flow is essential to redesign, and any effort to analyze work flow is about asking questions (Hofmann, 1993). The question is the key to:

- identifying customers.
- deciding what customers want and need.
- acknowledging performance in supplying customers with the products they want.
- recognizing and altering paradigms and algorithms to produce the outcomes customers want.
- ultimately drawing a project plan in a customer-satisfying frame.

Each step of the process of work flow analysis and redesign is based on continually asking questions in order to test for external and internal customer satisfaction. A question is often answered with another question. This is the process of analysis, and this is the process of redesign.

FIGURE 5.1 Sequential Steps for Critical Path Development

FOCUS PHASE:

   Is There An Issue/Concern/Problem?

ANALYZE PHASE:

   Why Is This Happening Or Not Happening And How?

DEVELOP PHASE:

   What Can We Do?

EXECUTE PHASE:

   When Can We Fix It? And Who Can Do It?

IDENTIFYING ALL Customers

Analysis regarding the **customers** of your product is the cornerstone to knowing if what you are doing is effective. Knowing who needs to be satisfied with your service or product and who may be touched, even tangentially, by the delivery of your product is vital (Figure 5.2).

FIGURE 5.2 Customer Identification

Who is my customer?

Who **needs** what I'm doing, making, providing?

Who **wants** what I'm doing, making, providing?

Who **uses** what I'm doing, making, providing?

Who **gets touched by** what I'm doing, making, providing?

Hidden Customers

Obviously for nurses on the delivery side of health care, the patient is the primary customer of services. The patient requires the service or product of the nurse directly. But there are hidden customers of nursing services as well, and they may be a number of the high-volume recipients of work flow by-products. These hidden customers are internal customers of nursing services—other nurses, physicians on staff, radiology services personnel, social workers, medical records clerks, billing and finance workers, and pharmacy and laboratory technicians—and may outnumber the patient and the patient's family two or three to one.

Forbes Health System in Pennsylvania instituted a program for patients admitted with a diagnosis of pneumonia. The program called for these patients to have essential diagnostic studies done quickly upon presentation and for therapy to be instituted promptly. In a program review, Forbes found quick nursing assessment combined with early intervention by diagnostic service personnel led to a decrease in patient mortality. But the patient who benefited from early diagnostic results and therapy institution was not the *only* customer of the nursing staff. Respiratory therapists, doctors, and others in the patient care loop were also customers. As is true whenever multidisciplinary services are delivered, the work team members were each others' customers in many instances. They were hidden customers (Figure 5.3) (McGarvey & Harper, 1993).

The hidden customers on the work team at Forbes were identified by looking at the admission protocol and asking "Which professionals deliver the service?" and "Who is affected by what another health care worker orders, supplies, reports, delivers?" (Figure 5.4).

Internal Versus External Customers

Questioning is the key to analyzing work flow and designing change. It is the key as well to identifying customers—all customers. So far we have looked at identifying internal customers as opposed to the patient who receives nursing skills first hand. We have focused on the work team member whose own service is affected by other services provided to the patient.

To determine who beside the patients are external customers, ask, "Who outside this clinic [hospital, emergency department, etc.] is affected by what I do for my primary internal customer, my patient?" For example, is the community affected? Are the insurers affected? Lowered mortality rates will affect the public health of the community, the dollars expended by insurers, and the total health care dollars as reflected by a percentage of the gross national product. Clearly the community and the insurers are external customers.

TIP

When you know your customer, you can design or redesign your service to increase effectiveness.

Every time you examine service, product, and work flow, it is important to identify all the customers—internal and external, primary and secondary—in order to evaluate the potential impact for a positive outcome. Identifying customers is step 1 in analyzing work flow.

IDENTIFYING IMPORTANT ASPECTS OF CARE, CONSTRUCTING INDICATORS, AND SETTING THRESHOLDS

After beginning the process of identifying customers, step 2 in analyzing work flow is identifying what important services or products are being supplied and then documenting how well, how timely, and how completely services or products are being supplied.

FIGURE 5.3 Identifying All the Customers

The customer/the hidden customer

The customer	The hidden customer
Patient	Physician
	Radiology technician
	Nurse
	Patient's family
	Social worker
	Admitting clerk
	Pharmacy
	Lab

FIGURE 5.4 Considering All the Customers

On Admission Protocol	Health Care Professional Involved	Who Affects Who?
A. Obtain sputum cultures	Respiratory therapist, MD	Patient and MD affected by respiratory therapist's technical skill
Respiratory therapist to obtain		
Two attempts/second with stimulation		
Bronchoscopic collection as a last resort by MD request		
Grams stain to confirm sputum before culturing		
B. Draw blood cultures	Lab technician, RN, MD	Respiratory therapist, lab technician, RN, MD affected by patient cooperation
Two times on all patients		
C. Administer antibiotics within four hours	Etc.	Etc.
If timely cultures cannot be obtained, antibiotics anyway		
D. Cover Mycoplasma and Legionella		
Strongly suggested		
E. Pulmonary/infectious disease consult		
Encourage, if patient has not improved within 48 hours		

A number of years ago I worked the night shift in a convenience store. At each change of shift, there was a ritual that required the full attention of the oncoming and departing clerks. Each clerk independently counted and recorded the amount of money in the cash register. The totals had to match. It was not good enough to hold the pennies in your hand and say, "It feels like 42 cents." Each clerk had to count each penny and account for every coin and bill in the cash register, and each had to verify the other's count. The process of evaluation for health care is the same as counting pennies in the till.

TIP

Identifying important aspects of care, constructing indicators, and setting thresholds is the process by which a nurse knows if she or he is providing the service or product that the customer wants and needs.

We cannot assume success or assume the end product is flawless just because we follow protocols, policies, and procedures. Nor can we assume that patients are being effectively treated. Likewise, we cannot be sure that our customer has been effectively helped by our efforts toward the same goal within a particular pathway of care delivery. We must count the pennies.

The simplest formula for knowing how we are doing at delivering care or service is to outline the important **aspect of care** or service we believe we are providing, to construct an **indicator** to show if we are providing the service, and then to set a **threshold** for performance. Once again the question is key in this process (Figure 5.5).

Aspects of care, indicators, and thresholds have been important tools in the quality improvement process for several years because they provide a way to measure what we think we are providing for our customers: patients, physicians, other health care professionals, and the community. These tools help in analyzing the end product or the by-products along the way. To say how many pennies are in the till or in health care delivery, to be able to know if we are providing what our patients want and need, we can ask these questions:

- What is important about what I do for the patient? *(aspect of care)*
- How will I know I am doing it? *(indicator)*
- What is acceptable performance? *(threshold)*

FIGURE 5.5 Aspects of Care Indicators and Thresholds

Who is my customer?

Internal   External

What's an important service/product I provide?

I Do this:
1.
2.
3.

How will I know I'm providing it?

Because:
1.
2.
3.

What's acceptable performance?

For my customer?   For me?
1.   1.
2.   2.
3.   3.

Flemming (1993) reported some important indications of appropriate outcomes of treatment for hip fracture in a skilled nursing facility (SNF):

1. No decubitus ulcer formation during SNF stay.
2. No contractural deformity during SNF stay.
3. No dislocation of surgical hip repair during SNF stay.
4. Appropriate weight-bearing status maintained during SNF stay.
5. Patient, staff, and family taught appropriate hip precautions.
6. All short-term goals on physical therapy (PT) initial evaluation achieved.
7. All long-term goals on PT initial evaluation achieved.
8. Home care program taught, or home health referral made when indicated; staff instructed in maintenance-level program if patient remains as a long-term resident.

Each one of these may be translated into an important aspect of care. And for each important aspect of care we can develop an indicator and a threshold by asking and answering the questions. For example, for indication 4 in the previous list, the following questions, and their answers could be developed:

Important aspect of care: *What is important about what I do or provide?* It is important that I help all my hip fracture patients retain appropriate weight-bearing status.

Indicator: *How will I know I am doing that?* Each hip fracture patient will leave the SNF at or above the weight-bearing goal set by the physician/physical therapist.

Threshold: *What is an acceptable level of success?* Ninety percent of all my hip fracture patients will leave the SNF at or above the weight-bearing goal set on admission.

Once the important aspects of care, indicators, and thresholds can measure the effectiveness of interventions, the positive or negative impact of work flow can be analyzed. Following are changes that will affect the work flow. Customer-driven management and total quality management are complete when we effectively and continuously provide needed services (Figure 5.6).

AREAS WHERE WORK FLOW CHANGES ARE NEEDED

- **To improve the care or service.**
- **To improve the outcome.**
- **To match the expectations of the customer more closely.**

FIGURE 5.6 Customer-Driven Quality Management

Identifying customer expectations and
determining professional standards

Translating expectations and standards into
operational procedures

Measuring/checking and
remeasuring and **rechecking**

Analyzing work flow for patient-customer satisfaction is the process of identifying expectations, determining the nursing standards that will facilitate meeting those expectations, and translating expectations and standards into procedures that produce desired outcomes. Ultimately, measuring and checking and remeasuring and rechecking how well patient and other customer expectations are met allows further refinement of work flow.

BENCHMARKING

Benchmarking for moving beyond the status quo is the current best practice or the most acceptable practice pattern. At what level are we supplying a satisfying service? Analysis of benchmarks helps determine whether outcomes and products match customers' needs as well as professional standards and personal health care biases. "By definition," writes Olmstead (1993), "benchmarking is a self-improvement process that compares and measures organizations' processes against those of other organizations." But on an individual, unit, or service level, it is a way of getting at the question of whether the appropriate services and outcomes are being delivered at the level of expectation. After step 1 of analyzing work flow—identifying customers—and step 2—constructing indicators and thresholds to measure effectiveness—benchmarking is the logical next step.

THE STEPS OF BENCHMARKING

1. **Collect data.**
2. **Track and trend.**
3. **Eliminate Sentinel Events (see page 77).**
4. **Identify the exceptional care/service/product.**
5. **Acknowledge any "not where we want to be" outcomes.**
6. **Challenge for change.**

Collecting Data, Tracking, and Trending

Once the thresholds for indicators to be measured are developed, data collection should occur in a periodic manner based on one of the following:

- employee work schedules
- frequency of particular nursing interventions

- availability of presenting candidates for measurement
- a fixed periodic schedule (hourly, daily, weekly, etc.)

The importance of the data collected will be reflected through tracking and trending. As the database grows, the trends more accurately reflect the real delivery of care or service. Figure 5.7 shows two indicators/thresholds tracked and trended over 6 months. Note that although Indicator I is reported monthly, the sponge and needle count match can be logged daily, weekly, or monthly. Real counts are documented at every surgical closing, thus allowing for immediate intervention if the counts are wrong. Tallying the percentage of matches can be postponed. **Sentinel events** are those in which the counts are wrong and are recognized and acted upon immediately; these events identify one-time exceptions to standards of care or service and usually are noted quickly because they may trigger adverse outcomes. Trends such as decreases in the percentage of matches over time, on the other hand, are evaluated at set intervals. Trends show failure to achieve threshold over time. By tracking and trending variations in compliance or match, one is alerted to question operational procedures in the operating room, compliance with procedures, individual compliance, and so forth. Trending shows if a particular procedure or person is outside expectation repeatedly.

Indicator II, on the other hand, is best collected at least daily, allowing for quick intervention if something exceptional is discovered (for example, a brittle diabetic has not been nutritionally evaluated and an appropriate diet ordered). While it may be reported monthly, the daily or at least weekly collection allows for nursing staff to identify exceptional (outside the expected) care or service. These exceptional cases may then be recognized and addressed before the patient is compromised or perhaps discharged without the full benefit of available medical intervention. A sentinel event associated with Indicator I is noted at the time of service, whether or not the indicator exhibits or whether or not you are tracking the matches. Adverse outcomes associated with Indicator II, on the other hand, are less likely to be identified until documentation is checked because this indicator identifies lapse in service rather than an inappropriately performed service.

Tracking and trending performance against thresholds over the long term graphically shows current practice and clearly illustrates any "not where we want to be" performance. Without these benchmarks of performance demonstrated by indicators and thresholds trended over time, one can only guess at how well the care and service is provided commensurate with the needs of patients and other customers.

FIGURE 5.7   Data Trending over Six Months for Two Indicators

---

Indicator I: Pre-Op and Post-Op sponge and needle counts match.

Threshold: 100%

	Jan	Feb	Mar	Apr	May	June
# Cases	92	112	97	98	104	79
% Match	100	100	100	100	100	100

Indicator II: Patient weights, nutrition needs assessments and action plans.

A. Weights are obtained on all patients within 24 hours of admission or transfer,

and

B. Patients with comorbid diagnoses of congestive heart failure, coronary heart disease, diabetus mellitus, or morbid obesity will have a nutrition needs assessment and an action plan documented within 48 hours of admission or transfer.

Patient Weights Threshold A: 100%

	Jan	Feb	Mar	Apr	May	June
# Cases	24	19	19	21	12	23
% Obtained	98	100	100	99	100	100

Patients with Comorbid Diagnoses Threshold B: 100%

	Jan	Feb	Mar	Apr	May	June
# Cases	14	9	11	12	9	17
% Assessment	86	100	91	92	100	100
% Plan	86	89	73	76	100	100

Measuring and Deciphering: Tracking, Trending, and Evaluating

Tracking patient care is more usual than monitoring how well needed services are supplied to other members of the work team. Figure 5.8 shows the trend of the nursing service's sending patient charts to the medical records and billing department in a timely fashion over a 3-month period but also breaks out more evaluative trends for a particular month in which nursing fell below the threshold.

FIGURE 5.8	Trending Services to Other Health Care Professionals

Major Aspect of Care or Service

It is important to get discharged/expired patients' records to Medical Records timely for coding and billing purposes.

Indicator

All discharged/expired patients' records will be sent to Medical Records no later than 1 hour after the close of shift on which the patient was discharged or expired.

Threshold

90%

Jan	Feb	Mar	Apr	May	Jun	Jul	Aug	Sep	Oct	Nov	Dec
98	89	96									

	Feb		
	7-3	3-11	11-7
Med/Surg	70	94	100
Hem/Onc	72	92	100
Labor/Del	82	91	100
Nursery	87	95	100
Burn Unit	69	87	100

The February percentage of compliance for the indicator suggests several questions. By asking and answering the questions, work flow can be evaluated and redesign accomplished. If the major aspect of care or service remains important to provide at the target threshold, factors that may get in the way of reaching the target threshold must be examined. For example:

1. Are there differences of performance across shifts?
   - What is the staff-patient ratio on each shift? Does it matter?
   - What affects shift workload? Are there more administrative duties, more meetings that take staff off the floor?

- What leadership and secretarial support is available on each shift?
- Are all shifts using the same procedure?
2. Does the burn unit have unique issues?

Indicators and thresholds provide information about performance. Without measurement, without collecting data, we essentially hold up our handful of pennies and say, "It *feels* like 42 cents."

Benchmarks are tools to decipher where we are. Trending benchmarks and analyzing component parts begin the challenge of change. We begin to move toward increasing the match between expectation and outcome. We begin to move toward redesigning the organization, procedures, or services to provide what customers need and desire from health care professionals.

THE SIMPLEST TOOL: ASKING THE QUESTION

The fourth step in the process of analyzing work flow for ultimate change or redesign again is simply to ask the question.

Outcome Perspective

This step begins with the product or outcome. It asks:

- What is really happening?
- What is not happening?
- Is this OK with my patient [customer]?
- Is this OK with me?

These questions, which focus on the end product, are asked from the outcome perspective.

Production Perspective

If we begin to ask questions about who is doing what or how something is being done, we focus on the production perspective—for example:

- Who is making this happen?
- Who is keeping this from happening?
- When does this happen?
- How does this happen?

- Why does this happen?
- Does this need to happen?

Brainstorming to identify current practice for a procedure clarifies all the steps taken. Two models that consider aspects of production can be used to categorize steps. Pilgram (1993) constructed a fishbone diagram to track various influences on work product outcome (Figure 5.9). Starting from "Lab Test Initiated" and going to "Results Charted in a Timely Fashion," she chose to look at workforce, machines, methods, and materials.

FIGURE 5.9 Fishbone Diagram: Pathology Distribution Quality Action Team

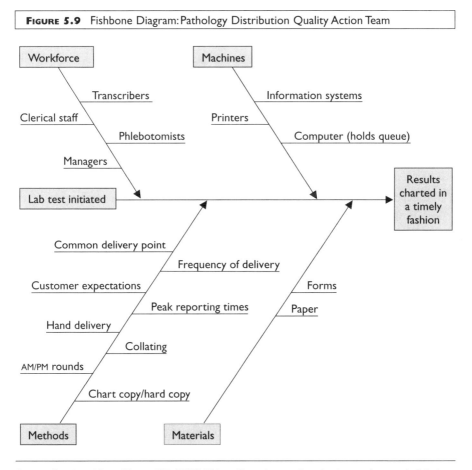

Source: Reprinted from Pilgram, P. B. (1993). Using a Team Approach to Implement Automatic Printing of Pathology/Radiology Reports. *Journal of Healthcare Quality, 15*(1), p. 30, with permission of the National Association for Healthcare Quality, 5700 Old Orchard Road, First Floor, Skokie, IL 60077-1057. Copyright ©1993 National Association for Healthcare Quality.

Kaminski (1992) showed different parameters for her "Diagram of Cause Theories" when she reported the work of a managed care–emergency department team charged with the "mission to increase patient, staff, and physician satisfaction by streamlining the care and disposition process as it relates to managed care and making a better match between the patient and the on-call referral specialist." Coming off her fishbone or diagram of cause continuum were these components:

- politics
- environment
- people
- education
- information
- procedures/policies

When one can recognize the forces that have an impact on outcome, one can begin to chart the complete flow of activity from expectation to outcome, from vision to product. For each segment or division of the impacting force along the fishbone diagram or continuum, one can chart the flow of work or service delivery to the final outcome or final product.

Sticky Note Approach

An easy way to chart current work flow and encourage brainstorming improvements simultaneously is to use individual pieces of paper with single function labels. Instead of writing titles and labels on a single sheet of paper with arrows going from one boxed label to another to indicate the flow of steps, the "sticky note approach" allows easy movement of labels to visualize change. As opportunities for change in flow are identified, the notes can be shifted from one spot to another or discarded. The steps for getting changed medication orders to the pharmacy, filled, and back to the floor with the quickest turnaround is graphically represented in Figure 5.10. Other work flow opportunities can be identified visually by rearranging the notes in the "what-if" column. Each step is an opportunity for error and delay. Clearly, taking one step out of the process or adding one step to it alters the outcome in efficacy, effectiveness, and timeliness.

TIP

Simplifying a process eliminates opportunities for errors and delay.

FIGURE 5.10 Identifying the Quickest Turnaround Time

As Is		Time		What If	
MD	Orders on order sheet				Orders on computer (electronic signature)
Ward clerk	Orders off order sheet into computer	+	MD		Computer print out of order • on floor • in pharmacy
RN	Medication order change signed off				
Pharmacist	Orders received in pharmacy	++	Pharmacist	Medications dispensed by pharmacy	Orders charted
	Medications dispensed by pharmacy				Ward clerk
Messenger	Medications picked up from pharmacy	+++	Messenger	Medications picked up from pharmacy	Medication order signed off
RN	Medications received on floor	++++	RN	Medications received on floor	RN
	Medications set up on med cart			Medications set up on med cart	
	Medications given to patient	+++++		Medications given to patient	

Initiation Perspective

Once the current work flow is established and the desired work flow is recognized, an initiation perspective becomes key. Among the questions that naturally arise are these:

- How realistic are the changes we want to see?
- How will these changes work?
- Who can authorize the changes?
- What things cannot change?
- Are the "can't change" items valid?
- Why this?
- Why not this?

Philosophic Perspective

From this ongoing questioning comes the opportunity to improve through change and redesign. The simplest tool, the question, may also be the most painful tool. The question that challenges the philosophic approach to care delivery—"why this way and not that way?" or "why this service and not that service?"—tends to frighten even the most sincere customer advocates. But work flow must be based on the customer and, of course, on the outcome or product that the patient or other customer wants and needs rather than on tradition. To provide the best care, to seize the opportunity to improve in care and service delivery, tough, philosophically challenging questions must be asked and answered. How many times have we heard, if not muttered ourselves, "This just goes against how we were taught to care for our patient," or "This is just the opposite to what we've always done"? Without daring to question, to rethink, to risk throwing the baby out with the bathwater, and to challenge philosophic tradition we may not be able to redesign processes for quality improvement. A philosophic perspective must be entertained. Why *not* a new approach? Why *not* a different direction? These questions are perhaps the simplest, and toughest, ones of all.

GETTING OUT OF THE BOG

Giving ourselves permission to put aside tradition to accomplish the task of meeting customers' needs is the key to redesigning work flow and improving quality. Tools must change. Mental, value-based tools help to accomplish this change. It is time to give up or change our paradigms, algorithms, sacred territories, and views of stewardship. The old rules of the game and the consistency and comfort they afford are the paradigm that must be supplanted with a new perspective. The old algorithms that tell us, "if this, then that," need updating. The new algorithms may seem foreign and may give others some power we previously exercised, but without new paradigms, a redesigned organization cannot evolve. If old algorithms and paradigms do not move us toward the product we want, we must invest in new paradigms. For the health care professional, stewardship rests on staying attuned to patients' needs and expectations. Stewardship rests on examining the outcomes of care and service.

William Arnold (1993) has said that "quality improvement is truly an inside-out process. People in organizations no longer want to play dress rehearsal, and our approach toward work needs to be one of learning how to let go of some old, useless ideas rather than one of grabbing hold of a fancy new idea. This letting-go process can be achieved by education." By replacing our fears with information, we can meet the challenge of change and redesign organizations, products, and systems to improve the quality of how we serve.

Liftoff

According to Rosabeth Moss Kanter (1983), the climate of success in an organization is based on the:

- emotional and value commitment between person and organization
- company's culture (whether it pushes tradition or change)
- culture of pride, the recognition of past successes

Ellen Gaucher (1992), in a presentation at the JCAHO's fifth annual National Forum on Health Care Quality Improvement, explained the management shift for total quality management (TQM) as a shift from conventional to transformational (Figure 5.11).

Clearly, moving from traditional and stable to different and unconfirmed requires an emotional and creative leap forward. The culmination of all the tools of questioning we have explored thus far in this chapter is the certain knowledge that change is necessary, can happen, is not a marker of past failures, and does now and will continue to challenge us.

Here we are today. We are on a continuum of "time now." Dispersed along the continuum are our customers, ourselves, and our products. We all are continually changing, evolving, and improving.

How do we become comfortable with this change toward improvement? How do we visualize change, and, ultimately, how do we make change?

FIGURE 5.11   Leadership for Total Quality Management

From Conventional to Transformational Leadership

Exclusive strategic planning	$\rightarrow$	Sharing mission/vision strategies and planning
Minimizing risks	$\rightarrow$	Mastering change
Maximizing profits	$\rightarrow$	Serving the customers
Maintaining equilibrium	$\rightarrow$	Managing diversity
Managing staff	$\rightarrow$	Coaching, counseling, and empowering staff

Source: Courtesy of Ellen J. Gaucher.

Draw It Upside Down First

This simple exercise is designed to make your right brain work and increase your creativity. The exercise is to put an object in front of you and to draw it as if it were upside down. This exercise increases creative powers tremendously because it stretches you to view things from a new perspective. As I have worked with groups to help them make changes and to move from one organizational structure to another, I have used this technique to stretch the participants' sense of things. Give yourself the edge on creative thinking and perspective by trying to look at familiar things in new ways.

Keep It Simple

One of the biggest traps we all fall into is the trap of complications. It comes about as an honest desire to do it all and to do it all now. As you move toward redesign, keep it simple by adhering to guiding principles. The elaborate may be comfortable because it fogs the outcome and imparts a sense of activity. But a simple, direct approach with clear end points helps everyone stay focused on the point of the change, the point of the effort, and the expectation of the patient or other customer.

Let It Be the Way It Is

If there are parts of a system that make functional sense or just plain work to provide the desired outcome, keep them—even if you think the wrong people are doing them. Keep them or institute them even if they fall outside the traditional order. Let it be the way it is. Functional outcome is a strong indicator that the process, whether it is a new or an old one, is working. Just as tradition sometimes limits our vision, innovation sometimes prohibits use of old processes even though they are effective. Leave effective processes alone until the forces of change balance. Success with meeting patient- and other customer-focused outcomes will balance with the fear of change over time.

A Package of Services, a Package of Care Delivery

James Brian Quinn in *Intelligent Enterprise: A New Paradigm for A New Era* (1992) has said we need "to reconceive every organization as packages of interdependent services." So it is with nursing and all other contributors to health care delivery. Isolated actions with the best of intent, with patient satisfaction and positive outcome as the focus, have the opportunity to miss the mark if we forget our hidden customers: everyone on the work flow team. We are indeed each packages of interdependent services, and we need to complement and facilitate one another's actions. Changes in one area do affect other interdependent parts of the system. We have to understand our structural complexities and reduce the barriers to team efforts and effectiveness (Murphy, 1993).

SUMMARY

The nursing process is characterized by assessment, planning, implementation, and evaluation (Sullivan & Decker, 1992). It is the process of asking questions at every point of the way. The question is the key to translating patient expectations and nursing standards into procedures that produce desired outcomes. Redesign is no different from using the nursing process on a broader scale. The questions we should repeatedly ask are these:

- Who are my customers?
- What are the important aspects of care or service they want or need?
- How will I know I am providing them?
- How well, how often, and at what level do I want to provide the care or other service?

These questions work to identify barriers to change and opportunities to increase effectiveness regardless of who the customer is. Internal and external customers may be affected beneficially if we base our work product and any redesign on continually checking and rechecking who the customers are, what it is they want, and what it is we are providing:

- What is important about what I do?
- How will I know I am doing it?
- At what level do I want to do it?

Patient-focused care looks at complaints naturally, but patient-focused care moves beyond to search out new ways to streamline services. Continuous quality improvement teams ask questions. They examine how they do things. They survey patients, doctors, and staff. And they implement change (Bovender, 1993).

A question is often answered with another question. This is the process of analysis and this is the process of redesign. This is the process of quality improvement (Figure 5.12).

FIGURE 5.12   The Nursing Process Applied to Analyzing Work Flow

The Nursing Process	Analyzing Work Flow	

Assessment

Start with the Questions

Who are my customers?

What do they want and need?

How will I know I'm providing these?

> * Important aspects of care/service
> * Indicators
> * Thresholds

Planning

Measure and Check

> * Track and trend
> * Benchmark

Implementation

Perspective for Change and Changing Perspectives

Outcome perspective

Production perspective

Initiation perspective

Philosophic perspective

> * Draw it upside down
> * Keep it simple
> * Let it be the way it is

Evaluation

Start Again with the Questions

Who are my customers?

What do they want and need?

How will I know I'm providing these?

REFERENCES

Arnold, W. (1993). The leader's role in implementing quality improvement: Walking the talk. *Quality Review Bulletin, 19*(3), 79–82.

Bovender, N. P. (1993). Forming "hospitals within hospitals" to ensure better and more cost-effective care. *Quality Matters, 2*(5), 23–25.

Flemming, P. (1993). Improving outcomes in hip fracture patients: Using QA tools in a skilled nursing facility physical therapy clinic. *Journal for Healthcare Quality, 15*(4), 21–24.

Gaucher, E. (1992). The evolutionary stages of leadership in a total quality organization. Presentation to fifth annual national forum on health care quality improvement. Chicago, IL: JCAHO

Hofmann, P. A. (1993). Critical path method: An important tool for coordinating clinical care. *Journal of Quality Improvement, 19*(7), 235–246.

Kaminiski, G. (1992). Total quality management at Bethesda, Inc. *Journal of Healthcare Quality, 14*(6), 38–53.

Kanter, R. M. (1983). *The change masters: Innovation and entrepreneurship in the American corporation.* New York: Simon & Schuster.

McGarvey, R. N., & Harper, J. J. (1993). Pneumonia mortality reduction and quality improvement in a community hospital. *Quality Review Bulletin, 19*(4), 124–130.

Murphy, E. C. (1993). Reengineering for quality: How to build a patient-focused hospital. *Quality Matters, 2*(4), 26–27.

Olmstead, R. V. (1993). Benchmarking: A method of improving health care processes by "just asking for them." *Quality Matters, 2*(2), 26–27.

Pilgram, P. B. (1993). Using a team approach to implement automatic printing of pathology/radiology reports. *Journal of Healthcare Quality, 15*(1), 29–33.

Quinn, J. B. (1992). *Intelligent enterprise: A new paradigm for a new era.* New York: Free Press.

Sullivan, E. J., & Decker, P. J. (1992). *Effective management in nursing.* Redwood City, CA: Addison-Wesley.

Sullivan, E. J., & Decker, P. J. (1993). Meeting update: Leading the transformation in health care quality through improved performance, JCAHO's fifth annual national forum on health care quality improvement. *Quality Review Bulletin, 19*(2), 67–68.

CHAPTER 6

Project Development

Today's hospitals are in danger of becoming what Alvin Toffler (1985) calls "organizational dinosaurs." Some have lost the ability to respond quickly to change, both internal and external. Their very survival is challenged by competitors that are more responsive. Hospitals can survive if they meet new challenges.

A strong **customer focus** provides distinct advantages. By redefining value to its customers, an organization increases customers' expectations beyond the competition's reach (Treacy & Weirsema, 1993). Of course, the ability to deliver on promises and to maximize value-added operations is critical to achieving a competitive edge.

A formal project approach supports the management of rapid change and thus facilitates an organization's ability to compete. It is the vehicle by which redesign occurs. The best resources of the organization can be combined in a project format to allow broad participation in the major changes implied by redesign. Such broad-based decisions are not made in isolation and are less likely to be repealed later due to operational and political realities.

TIP

Assess group culture prior to change and then customize strategies.

An organization's culture can be the most relevant factor concerning the success or failure of redesign (Coeling & Simms, 1993a). Culture is not static across an organization; two groups affected by a change, for example, may react from quite different perspectives. With an appreciation of culture's role comes the wisdom to customize project strategies for consistent outcomes across a variety of change situations (Coeling & Simms, 1993b).

The larger issue of how many projects can be managed successfully must be addressed. The need to make numerous fundamental changes must be balanced with the availability of resources and the adaptive capacity of the workforce. A successful approach to managing overall change is with **aggregate project planning** (Wheelwright & Clark, 1992). This mapping process helps administrations to plan project types and time lines consistent with strategic planning and work capacity constraints. In this way, resources are committed only to projects that are central to the organization's best interests.

PROJECT DEFINED

A **project** is an organizational strategy to achieve change through specific goal attainment within a limited time frame. As an organizational strategy, a project can pull together targeted human resources from across the institution to form a temporary work group for the purpose of completing a project. In addition to the obvious benefit of completing specific project goals, the organization benefits through human resource members, as well as through improved organizational communication added by new networks developed during the project.

TIP

A well-managed project employs strategies to limit the scope of activities and to control risks associated with change.

The specific goals that focus a project may encompass quality, cost, and operational aspects. These goals must reflect the processes and outcomes desired to resolve the underlying problem or issue that initiated the project. An orderly, detailed list of activities required to achieve change within prescribed time lines is the main management tool for successful projects. The process by which a project is approved within the organization also ensures that the project will use strategies appropriate to the organization's culture and mission.

At what level of complexity simple change management becomes a more formal project will differ according to institutional definitions but generally centers on how many resources are required to complete the change. A formal project may be undertaken when the change requires resources that span departments or divisions of the organization, or when change is unfamiliar, complex, or risky (Marriner-Tomey, 1988). Also, when the amount of time or material resources exceed a predetermined level, a formal project process may be triggered. Generally if more than 50 hours and more than $5,000 will be required, some level of project plan may be required.

FIVE PHASES OF PROJECTS

1. conceptual phase
2. structural phase
3. process phase
4. completion phase
5. maintenance phase (Davis, 1992)

The conceptual phase includes brainstorming about the problem and all possible choices for solution. Political and philosophical issues must be addressed before you can move on to the next phase, the structural phase. The project is more clearly defined in this second phase through addressing tactical and operational concerns. The project is "roughed in" in outline form, using the project planning outline or some other format. In the third phase, the process phase, the people part of the plan is designed. What happens in this phase is critical to the acceptance of change and, ultimately, the success of the plan. The completion phase is the actual implementation of the plan. Adequate resources are needed to ensure a smooth implementation. The maintenance phase includes "fine tuning" of the change, enculturation of the change, and ongoing evaluation.

TYPES OF PROJECTS

Several types of projects are found within complex organizations, and each type requires specific approaches tailored to its unique nature. Table 6.1 summarizes key approaches to use with specific project types.

TABLE 6.1 Project Types and Key Approaches

TYPES	ISSUES	STRATEGIES
Innovations (e.g., new product development, operational changes, new organizational approaches, patient-focused redesign)	Are major transformations	Require creativity, insight into customer needs
		Must think outside of current context
	Turf issues may lead to defeat	May need consultant to help
		Ensure essential information and services with political pull.
	Need political pull from top	Select high-ranking steering committee
		Support departments threatened by changes
Major system change (e.g., implementing emerging technologies, such as upgrading a computer system)	Project has broad impact	Need representation of all constituents
		Timing of project components important
		Training considerations critical
		Additional support for transition needed
Problem focused Solution known (e.g., correcting regulatory deficiencies)	Complexity varies greatly	May not need formal project plan
		Can immediately focus on solution
	May be treating symptom	Ensure real problem is identified
		May need outside help with problem identification
Solution unknown (e.g., quality improvement projects)	Complex; requires formal project processes	Team must investigate issues, recommend possible solutions
		Steering committee may help at key decision points

NEED FOR PROJECT MANAGEMENT

Why not simply let managers do their jobs without going through a formal project management process? The answer to that question rests with the impact of change on an organization. Major change is occurring in organizations at an ever-accelerating pace. Many times it is not just what is done that has the potential to create chaos. The "how" of change greatly affects the success of an operation. Ask any manager who has seen a major change create labor-relations problems that led to unionization. Hindsight in that kind of situation could lead the manager to do things very differently. Negative response to change can be minimized by the careful planning, communication, and coordination required by the project management process.

BENEFITS OF A FORMAL PROJECT PLAN

1. **Provides structure for project**
   - Detailed plan ensures proper sequence and timing of change.
   - Details are agreed on up front with approval process.
   - Disciplined structure of plan keeps all facets in control.
2. **Ensures focus and resources**
   - Limits focus and keeps team on tasks at hand.
   - Resources are approved with plan.
3. **Sets time frames and benchmarks**
   - Tools (e.g., Gantt charts, PERT charts, task lists, manpower utilization matrices, progress reports) ensure time frames are met. (These are discussed in detail in Chapter 7.)
   - Benchmarks may be critical activities or quality indicators that ensure proper problem resolution.
4. **Defines contract for change**
   - Project is consistent with culture and vision of organization.
   - Sign-off system means content and process meet standards to limit risks and ensure success.

RESOURCES FOR CHANGE

The human resources needed to carry off a major project can be staggering, and once the organization commits those resources, it has a vested interest in the outcome. The project team and any other people involved are being diverted from their usual activities. Functional managers may hesitate to release their best staff to a project. Productivity can be affected by a major project, so resources should not be committed lightly. Selection of a compatible team with a variety of skills ensures that the project is given the best chance for success.

TIP

Projects consume many types of resources, so it is important that projects reflect the strategic plan of the organization and receive proper administrative support.

Selection of the project manager (PM) is critical to the success of the project. The leadership skills needed by the PM are **critical thinking**, coordination, conflict management, delegation, communication, positive use of personal power, and attention to detail. The interpersonal approach taken by the PM is pivotal to success because conflict is inherent in change. The PM's role is to move the team through conflicts in a positive manner. A win-win approach requires skillful negotiation. Because dysfunctional behavior must be dealt with consistently and quickly, the PM must not be averse to confronting conflict directly.

Coordination is a major effort of any project, so communication becomes a key to effective resource utilization. A communication plan for the project should consider **internal integration**—the team building necessary for an effective project work group—and **external integration**, which considers necessary communication links with customer groups outside the team (Wesley & Easterling, 1991).

The team needs to meet at required intervals to ensure that subcommittees and small work groups are putting their efforts together for a larger effect than they would have individually. Conflict management skills become important if the group is to resolve issues and grow as a team.

Communication to the larger organization is needed to keep associates appraised of ongoing changes. Resources to ensure communication include existing tools such as company newsletters and other internal media systems. Sometimes a major project requires its own communication system—perhaps a limited-edition news approach, an in-service program, steering committees, staff meetings, or personal contact with key customers.

Documentation becomes important to communicate the process and status of the project. Minutes of meetings, updated flowcharts, and status reports are needed to leave a paper trail so that future change need not repeat some of the lessons learned in this project. Care must be exercised to ensure that production elements are shared with other projects so that duplication of efforts does not occur.

In addition to the human element, the project has physical requirements. Meeting places, often in limited supply, are needed to coordinate efforts. Some projects actually center on changes in the physical layout of an area. The lost opportunity costs for the space needs of the project should be calculated into the project budget.

Projects are by definition time limited. Time is money in the truest sense because the time required to complete a project is time diverted from other productive efforts. Time must be controlled as much as other resources. The most efficient way of coordinating efforts saves time. Effective meetings move the team toward project completion more efficiently than do poorly run meetings. A project manager who effectively delegates tasks will achieve results more quickly than the project manager who feels he or she must personally complete all tasks. Leadership is the critical factor to limiting the resource utilization of projects.

All of these resources must be estimated in the project budget that accompanies the project plan approval process. Many companies have operations management or operations research departments that can assist the project manager in estimating budget needs. Some companies are sophisticated enough to require a pro-forma needs analysis or cost-benefit analysis for any major project proposal.

NEEDS ANALYSIS AND BUSINESS PLAN

The depth of the **needs analysis** required by a project may vary greatly depending on the complexity of issues related to redesign and organizational management practices. The processes discussed in depth in Chapter 5 are critical to understanding underlying issues regarding operational needs as well as to analyzing patient needs systematically.

TIP

The needs analysis should explore all possible alternatives.

A **business plan** is a detailed plan that addresses a project's financial feasibility. This level of analysis is usually undertaken with large projects that reflect new service ventures or great uncertainty. The plan describes the project's concept and objectives in light of the organization's strategic plan and mission. The product or service is carefully defined through a **market analysis**. The potential for growth of the business as well as customer and payer analysis are part of the market analysis. A **financial plan** is then detailed, including a "**break-even analysis**, a **cash-flow analysis** and the development of a set of **pro forma** financial statements" (Finkler & Kovner, 1993, p. 281).

The break-even point is equivalent to the minimum volume of the service needed for the organization not to lose money. The cash-flow analysis indicates the pattern of cash outlay and cash receivables that will determine how much financial investment is needed to seed the project. Pro forma financial statements propose the financial position of the project within specified time periods—generally by fiscal year projections. These detailed activities are entered into in order to guide the institution's decision-making process. Projects usually will rise or fall based on financial performance. Exceptions to this rule are projects central to the institution's mission that must be performed despite financial implications.

Problem Definition

One area that frequently does not receive the attention needed is problem identification. Without proper problem identification, a project is doomed to resolve only symptoms. (See "Questions to Aid in Problem Definition.") The broader the input is from the organization, the better are the chances that the underlying problem will be identified. Sometimes the added perspective of an outside consultant can assist in this difficult aspect of project management.

QUESTIONS TO AID IN PROBLEM DEFINITION

- **What tells us there is a problem?**
- **What capability or resource is lacking?**
- **What customers are affected by the problem, and how?**
- **What does the customer really need?**
- **What factors are contributing to this problem?**
- **How can we distinguish between the problem and its symptoms?**
- **How does this problem affect the strategic plan?**
- **What regulations are not met?**

- **Will the situation correct itself? Can action be delayed?**
- **What needs to be done to help associates view the problem constructively?**

Alternative Solutions

Creativity is important to prevent the team from considering only routine choices. Often the best approach is to work from the perspective of creating an ideal model rather than from solving an existing problem from the perspective of treating a current system. Such thinking breaks the team out of past constraints. Often a facilitator is needed to help the group with this process. Once the most viable alternatives are determined, narrowing the choices further requires a detailed analysis. (See "Questions to Consider for Selecting Alternative Approaches.")

QUESTIONS TO CONSIDER FOR SELECTING ALTERNATIVE APPROACHES

- **Which is most customer focused?**
- **Which best meets the guiding principles for the project?**
- **Which improves quality, efficiency, and access?**
- **Which is least disruptive?**
- **Which is consistent with our mission?**
- **Which is least costly?**
- **Which will provide consensus?**
- **Which has greatest overall benefit?**
- **Which approach is the simplest?**

PROJECT DESIGN

The work done in the needs analysis provides direction to the formal project plan. The components of this plan give a structure for the project manager to use in organizing the project design. Each area flows naturally from the preceding one, building on previous decisions. Once approved, the project plan becomes the performance contract for the project manager and the team. Figure 6.1 provides a sample format for a project plan. A sample project plan is presented in the chapter appendix. We will explore the components of the project plan in detail because understanding the process of project planning is vital to the success of the undertaking.

FIGURE 6.1 Project Plan. A comprehensive format for project planning is outlined.

Project Title:

Project Definition: Define current problem/issue/process. Tell what you plan to do and why it is needed. Who is the customer? What is your vision for the process? What is the outcome you want?

Project Objectives:
1.
2.
3.
4.

Foreseen Problems/Issues and Plan to Resolve Them:

Preferred Implementation Strategy(ies):

People Factor: List people who should be involved in the project and how you plan to enlist them. What organizational structure is needed by the project?

Place Factor: What physical location, other department, or resources are needed for this project?

Time Factor: Identify length of project, specific time needed for each phase. Complete tools as appropriate to project and attach.

Communication Plan: Indicate all vehicles you plan to use to keep customers involved and informed of the project's progress.

Internal:

External:

FIGURE 6.1 *continued*

Documentation Plan: List all forms of documentation needed to monitor progress of project. Include minutes, interim reports, and quality improvement documents.

Analysis Plan: What instruments are needed for analysis? What will the outcome criteria be and how will they be measured?

Cost Factor: Provide a budget for your project. Include pro-forma, needs analysis, or cost-benefit analysis as appropriate.

       Labor:

       Materials:

       Total costs:

       Costs/unit:

Sign-off:

       Date:_____

       Project Manager_____

       Department Head_____

       Administrator_____

Source: Courtesy of St. Vincent Hospital and Health Care Center, Educational Services Department, Indianapolis, IN.

Project Title

The title chosen for the project should reflect major aspects of the work to be undertaken. Sometimes the title will be a concept. In this case, the concept needs to be defined for the organization so that the words transcend their meaning to reflect the massive changes implied. St. Vincent Hospital in Indianapolis titled a major project *Care2001*, signifying a major initiative on patient-focused care. It encompasses both the physical and philosophical changes necessary to bring about a hospital operation with the patient as the center of activity.

Project Definition and Vision

Defining the project moves the project manager from the concept to an operational level. It requires decisions relative to who, what, where, when, and why.

When the project is very large and of a long-term nature, it is vital to develop operating principles that will guide the future evolution of the plan. For example, for the *Care2001* concept, one guiding principle was that all innovations would be initiated from a patient-centered perspective. Another was to limit the number of hospital associates that the patient would be exposed to in a day. These two principles forced decisions to allocate ancillary services on the unit level and cross-train direct caregivers to broaden the scope of skills they could offer patients. The patients' needs had to be analyzed to determine what direction this process would take. Because fundamental patient needs differed on each nursing unit, a cookbook approach to repeating redesign efforts across multiple units would not work.

The desired outcome must be considered in the project definition. This step leads the project manager to refine outcomes by writing project objectives.

Project Objectives

Objectives are the guiding statements to direct processes and outcomes of the project. They must be stated in measurable terms and relate directly to the project definition and **guiding principles**. Consistency of thought is required to determine that each objective:

- is critical to the process and/or outcome of the project.
- is operationally possible to achieve.
- is coherent with the vision or mission of the project and the organization.
- considers technical and operational specifications needed for its completion.
- is written in specific, measurable, and often time-limited terms.

Foreseen Issues and Proposed Resolution

It is important to assess up front any problems that could arise as a result of the project. Organizations are political entities and as such require leaders who initiate change with open eyes. Consider major stakeholders and known turf issues. Are regulatory agencies going to be concerned about the changes that will result from this project? Is a certificate of need required by the state? If so, what political steps will be needed to secure approval for the project?

What resolutions to these issues are immediately apparent? These questions must be explored as the plan develops.

Preferred Implementation Strategy

This section entails outlining the broad implementation vision for the project. What approach to implementation seems appropriate for this project? Is further market research or a feasibility study needed as a first step in detailed project design? Should the project be piloted and, if so, where is the most likely site to facilitate the success of the project? How much associate participation will be sought for this project? The major detailed components of the implementation strategy are the people, places, deadlines, costs, communication and documentation aspects that encompass the remainder of the project plan format (Figure 6.1).

People Factor

The people factor will be pivotal to the success of the project. List specific people requested for the project due to their special expertise or their political clout. How do you plan to enlist these people? Consider how each person will fit into the overall team. Are they compatible? What roles will each person play? Ensure that all major constituencies are represented by the project team.

Frequently the outcome of the project will have an impact on the roles of certain categories of people. These people may be the forgotten workers of the organization who traditionally have not had a voice in change. They must be considered since the success of the project is tied to their ability and desire to perform new roles. What is the plan that will assist them to handle the change and develop any new skills needed? The leaders of the organization need to look beyond the obvious tasks of the new role to address underlying role needs. For example typically in health care work redesign, RNs' roles are broadened to include new tasks such as phlebotomy, electrocardiograms, and respiratory treatments. These new tasks are frequently shared with technical workers who also have been cross-trained. Roles blur because people tend to define their roles by what they do, not by their thought processes. What are the desired new relationships between these levels of workers? Who has the requisite knowledge and skill to direct patient care? These issues should be part of the initial vision of the project. If they are not kept central to the vision, organizations run the risk of not appreciating the knowledge worker because only tasks are considered in job design. The danger of this type of thinking in health care is that patient changes are often subtle and not readily detectable by technicians. The broader knowledge base of the RN is needed to assess for changes and intervene quickly to limit patient risk and organizational liability.

TIP

Build role clarification into the project planning process when roles will need to change. Remember the needs of knowledge workers.

The organizational structure necessary to support the project becomes an important decision point that affects the people engaged in the project. Will the project reside within a functional unit? Concern for the best interests of the project versus decisions favoring the functional group must be addressed.

The project structure possible with a matrix format allows for more autonomy of the project team. A more rapid response is possible with this format because project decisions do not have to filter through multiple department heads. Team members usually have two bosses in this format because they maintain their functional responsibilities in addition to team activities. Some models allow for team members to be loaned to the project full time, allowing for unity of command.

Clear lines of authority and reporting relationships must be agreed to at the start. For example, the depth and nature of a steering committee's role can be set by operating principles that clearly define areas of involvement and what decision points must be brought to the steering committee.

Place Factor

The place factor considers the project's physical needs. Is a temporary office or meeting room needed? Since space is at a premium at most facilities, this allocation is important. Other essential functions may need to be temporarily displaced. Moving costs for both the displaced area and the project team must be considered in the budget proposal. If the only space available is off-campus from the central facility, travel considerations must be addressed, because they affect productivity and costs.

Does this project entail a major renovation or building expansion plan? If so, this section becomes a major operational consideration and cost issue.

Time Factor

Projects are time limited by definition. A phased approach allows for proper timing of plan components. The work of the project is broken down into manageable units based on either the project objectives or timed phases of operation. The level of detail needed in this breakdown process is determined by the complexity of the project. The precise order of events is planned so that actions requiring precedent events are in proper order. The time needed to complete each activity is estimated using various project planning tools, discussed in detail later in this chapter.

Cost Factor

The organization is paying for the costs associated with the project. A central part of the decision to support or reject a project proposal is about whether resource consumption is warranted by anticipated outcomes and benefits. The extent to which the costs versus savings of a plan are known affects the relative risk of undertaking the project.

Generally, two major categories of costs are associated with projects. First, initial developmental costs must be considered. Costs can be assigned to the major objectives of the plan or to specific tasks and activities. This level of breakdown allows for decisions on modifying or eliminating aspects of the plan that are costly in relation to their expected benefit. (For the major components of developmental costs, see "Developmental Cost Categories.")

DEVELOPMENTAL COST CATEGORIES

1. **Labor**
   - Project team salaries and benefits
   - Research and technical support salaries and benefits
   - Advisory and administrative personnel salaries and benefits
   - Contracted services (consultants, temporary employees)
   - Training hours for faculty and students
2. **Supplies and equipment**
   - Purchase
   - Lease
   - Percentage of use of existing equipment

- Training supplies
- Communication costs
3. **Travel expenses**
4. **Space**
   - Temporary space costs
   - Moving costs for displaced areas and team
   - Allocated overhead
   - Missed opportunity

The second category for project budget consideration is that of ongoing operational costs. When the project is completed, what costs will recur as a result of the change? Also to be considered are the cost savings of a redesigned operation. Figure 6.2 provides a framework for analyzing the continuing operating costs for a project in relation to the current operation. Because innovation resulting from the project can improve efficiency or enhance marketability, costs per volume provides comparative figures. The volume can be length of stay, patient-days, procedures, quarter-hours (as in recovery room), or any other factor relevant for comparison.

Finally, the total costs of developmental and operational expenses must be considered. How long will the change need to be in effect to equal the costs of investment? What is the return on investment? Break-even analysis examines the income needed to break even on a project. The projected revenues (or vol-

FIGURE 6.2 Project Operating Cost Analysis

Category	Current Expenses	Projected Expenses
1. Full-time-equivalent personnel		
2. Salaries/benefits		
3. Overtime/on call		
4. Continuing education		
5. Travel		
6. Depreciation		
7. Maintenance		
8. Overhead		
9. Supplies		
10. Marketing		
Total costs		
Costs per volume		

ume of services) are compared to the total business expenses as discussed earlier (Busse, 1989). Calculations can be done in dollars or in units of service.

Communication Plan

Another key area to successful project planning is the communication plan. This section may not be required for small or relatively routine projects but is pivotal to complex and politically charged changes. Historical protocols, chain of command, and factors such as unions, turf battles, and board of trustee mission must be addressed. This plan should consider internal and external constituents.

TIP

How change is communicated can pave the way for acceptance or can block change.

Who are the internal constituents, and what is the best approach to meeting their information and participation needs? Many times one constituent group's needs will conflict with another's. The perfect example of this situation is the ongoing issues between physicians and nurses as to where patients' charts should be located. Nurses clearly prefer the charts at the point of use: the bedside. This location reduces nurses' duplication of work by allowing them to document on the record as opposed to trying to remember data or jotting them on work sheets. Many physicians, on the other hand, do not want to enter a patient's room before looking at the chart because they want to answer the patient's questions and have time to consider any problems identified in the record. Part of the communication plan in this example is to get the two groups to devise a solution that best meets everyone's needs. Will focus groups be the best process, or is a subcommittee needed to carry out more in-depth work? Who is the best facilitator in this situation? What are the political costs of the issue, and are those costs affordable? In other words, a calculated decision on which battles to wage may be part of the project communication plan.

The external communication plan may entail a detailed marketing plan or may simply list what agencies or people must be notified of changes and in what order. Targeting specific times or stages in the plan for communication is helpful. How will this be accomplished? Is a newsletter the best vehicle, or would direct contact be more advisable?

Documentation Plan

The process and outcomes of the project should be recorded in some permanent fashion to allow project monitoring as well as historical information. This documentation becomes especially critical when the project is a pilot for future change. In this case, it is extremely helpful for future change agents to appreciate the dynamics of previous projects' successes and failures. Minutes, interim reports, quality improvement monitors, new policies and procedures, educational curricula, and other forms of documentation should be listed in the documentation plan.

Analysis Plan

How will the markers of success be measured? In the planning stage, at least, the variables to be monitored should be listed. It is best if the instruments of evaluation are included. Analysis may be required for some aspect of the planning process. There may be a survey to determine needs that will direct project plan details or an assessment of laboratory utilization of a given patient population prior to determining what lab tests to decentralize. What resources are needed to analyze the data? What level of analysis will be performed? Is a statistician required?

It is important that these instruments be properly designed to measure what is intended in an unbiased way. For example, a survey of staff support for 12-hour shifts should be written so that it does not bias staff regarding the pros or cons of 12-hour shifts.

Written Sign-off

The project plan format should allow for written sign-offs. These lend power to the project team, suffice as performance contracts for project team members, and prevent miscommunication later in the change. Necessary negotiations to get agreement by important parties as to approach and concept for the plan must occur before too many organizational resources are consumed. At a minimum, the project manager, department head, and appropriate administrator should sign off.

Some institutions phase the sign-off procedure, with initial sign-off, mid-project sign-off, and sign-off at project completion. Another approach may be by project stages if subsequent stages depend on data obtained in earlier efforts.

TOOLS

Several tools are essential to successful project planning and implementation. They help to operationalize the broad definitions of a project into concrete, sequential steps needed to accomplish project objectives.

Gantt Chart

This tool, relatively easy to use, allows the project manager to outline the major components of the project along a time line extending through the expected length of the project. The amount of time needed for each activity and the exact dates for the activity to occur are graphed, with time placed horizontally and activities listed vertically, as seen in Figure 6.3. This

---

FIGURE 6.3   Gantt Chart. This chart outlines the same project depicted in Figure 6.2.

Activity	Weeks: 1	2	3	4	5	6	7	8	9	10	11	12	13
Plan approval		—											
Team/assignments		——											
Progress meetings		———————————————————————————————											
Objective 1:													
Focus groups		——											
Survey		————											
Data analysis			————										
Strategy formation				————									
Implementation						————————							
Evaluation												—	
Objective 2:													
Planning team development		——											
Select strategy		————											
Approve plan				——									
Implementation						———————————							
Evaluation												—	
Form steering committee	——												
Steering committee decision points				—		——						—	

---

pictorial representation helps the team to stay on target with its activities by providing a weekly or daily work list. The team can quickly see if it is on time or behind in the project. Gantt charts may be as complex or as simple as required by the project.

This is the best tool for the majority of projects due to its simplicity, visual representation, and ability to control the planning process. Having the Gantt chart completed prior to project approval leaves little doubt about the specifics of what will be done and when. This is especially important when the processes used in a project are as important as the outcomes desired.

Task Lists

Task lists attach responsibility to tasks, order the activities based on predecessor tasks, and identify the amount of time needed to complete tasks. Task lists do not provide a visual picture of the plan in the way Gantt charts do. Their main benefit is to detail tasks in projects where clearly identifying predecessors is vital such as in technical implementations. Figure 6.4 shows a sample task list format.

FIGURE 6.4 General Task List. A numbered, sequential list of major project tasks is identified, along with time frames and assignments.

ID #	Task	Predecessor	Time/Dates	Duty
1.	Plan approval		2 weeks	M.F.
2.	Select team/steering committee	1	1 day	M.F./J.D.
3.	Team assignments	2	5 days	M.F./J.D.
4.	Objective 1: Focus groups	3	10 days	S.L.
5.	Survey	3	15 days	D.C.
6.	Data analysis	4,5	15 days	S.L./D.C./B.M.
7.	Strategy formation	6	12 days	Team/Steering
8.	Implementation	7	25 days	Team
9.	Evaluation	8	5 days	Team/B.M.
10.	Objective 2: Planning team development	2,3	12 days	M.F./J.D./C.C.
11.	Select strategy	3	20 days	Team/J.D.
12.	Approve plan	11	5 days	Team/Steering
13.	Implementation	12	35 days	Team
14.	Evaluation	13	5 days	Team/B.M.

Note: Task lists would be broken down further for each major task on this list.

PERT Chart

Known as Project Evaluation and Review Technique, PERT charting is a refinement of the critical path method the U.S. military developed in the 1950s. When used to its fullest potential, PERT employs statistical probabilities to estimate the amount of time each project activity will consume (see Figure 6.5). Based on contingency theory, an average amount of time is estimated and then pessimistic and optimistic times are calculated based on standard deviations from the mean (Hermann, Alexander, & Kiely, 1992). If time lines are known for a number of activities, there is less likelihood of variance in the formula. The greater the uncertainty there is in the project, the less accurate PERT will be. Time changes required for one piece of the plan will have a cascading effect on the remainder of the project.

A major disadvantage to using the PERT system is the sophisticated mathematical modeling needed. Often computer analysis is required to monitor and update a PERT chart. The uncertainty of many organizational changes makes the use of this model superfluous.

Manpower Utilization Matrix

This planning tool estimates the amount of time required by all people involved in the project, whether team members or peripheral players. The purpose of this tool is to allocate FTEs (full-time equivalents) to the project by estimating the workload of everyone involved. This is vital to budgeting for the project. Secondary benefits to this level of planning are the assignment of work to specific people and the early identification of work inequity or overload based on phases of the plan. In such cases, need for additional help or joint responsibility among several people for key activities can be projected. Figure 6.6 shows a simple format for a manpower utilization matrix.

SUMMARY

Successful redesign efforts require mastery of the project planning process. Project planning, a managerial method to control risk inherent in change by ensuring that major changes are approved and well thought out, may be a very complex operation or the simplest approach to planning complex change.

The major areas for consideration in project planning were presented. The relative emphasis for the different sections of a project plan will vary

FIGURE 6.5 PERT Chart. Two PERT charts are shown for a sample project. The chart on the top depicts the flow of major project points. The bottom chart shows optimistic (average) and pessimistic time frames for each project point.

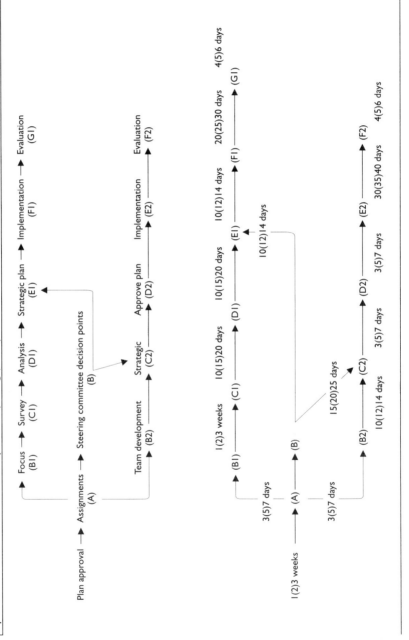

FIGURE 6.6 Sample from Manpower Utilization Matrix. The projected manpower hours of three team members for the project outlined in Figure 6.3 are listed along with completion dates.

Personnel	ID#	Task	Dates	Hours
M.F.	1	Plan approval	1/1–1/14	10
	2	Select team/steering committee	1/15	5
	3	Team assignments	1/16–1/21	25
	7	Strategy formation	2/21–3/3	30
	8	Implementation	3/4–3/30	120
	9	Evaluation	4/1–4/6	28
	10	Planning team development	1/15–2/1	40
	11	Select strategy	1/15–2/9	85
	12	Approve plan	2/9–2/14	12
	13	Implementation	2/15–3/30	165
	14	Evaluation	4/1–4/6	22
		TOTAL		570
J.D.	2	Selected team/steering committee	1/15	5
	3	Team assignments	1/16–1/21	8
	10	Planning team development	1/15–2/1	12
	11	Select strategy	1/15–2/9	20
		TOTAL		45
S.L.	4	Focus groups	1/15–1/25	40
	6	Data analysis	1/25–2/10	66
	7,8,9,11,12,13,14	Team	1/15–4/6	220
		TOTAL		326

depending on project need. For most applications, a project can be planned using the simple format in Figure 6.1. Not all sections of that format may be needed for a specific project. The project planning format can provide structure for enduring self-managed work teams as well as for short-term projects. Both are found in redesign. Self-managed work teams may engage in a series of projects and may benefit from a formal project plan structure.

The plan sets the stage for successful implementation, but there is much to consider in that area. The next chapter is devoted to implementing redesign.

REFERENCES

Busse, E. (1989). *The business plan: First step to success*. La Conned, WA: Holden Marketing Services.

Coeling, H., & Simms, L. M. (1993a). Facilitating innovation at the nursing unit level through cultural assessment, part 1: How to keep management ideas from falling on deaf ears. *Journal of Nursing Administration, 23*(4), 46–53.

Coeling, H., & Simms, L. M. (1993b). Facilitating innovation at the nursing unit level through cultural assessment, part 2: Adapting managerial ideas to the unit work group. *Journal of Nursing Administration, 23*(5), 13–20.

Davis, A. R. (1992). Project management: New approaches. *Nursing Management, 23*(9), 62–65.

Finkler, S. A., & Kovner, C. T. (1993). *Financial management for nurse managers and executives*. Philadelphia: W. B. Saunders.

Hermann, M. K., Alexander, J. S., & Kiely, J. (1992). Leadership and project management. In P. J. Decker & E. T. Sullivan (Eds.), *A micro/macro approach for effective nurse executives*. Norwalk, CT: Appleton & Lange.

Marriner-Tomey, A. (1988). *Guide to nursing management*. St. Louis: C. V. Mosby.

Toffler, A. (1985). *The adaptive corporation*. New York: Wiley.

Treacy, M., & Weirsema, F. (1993, January–February). Customer intimacy and other value disciplines. *Harvard Business Review*, 84–93.

Wesley, M. L., & Easterling, A. (1991). Improving clinical care through project management. *Nursing Administration Quarterly, 15*(4), 22–28.

Wheelwright, S. C., & Clark, K. B. (1992, March–April). Creating project plans to focus product development. *Harvard Business Review*, 70–82.

APPENDIX: SAMPLE PROJECT PLAN

Project Title:
Pilot of the Unit Support Assistant (USA) Role on Cardiac Medical

Project Definition: Define current problem/issue/process. Tell what you plan to do and why it is needed. Who is the customer? What is your vision for the process? What is the outcome you want?

The unit has been redesigned for a patient-focused approach that includes the addition of nurse servers. The USA role will assist the nursing personnel to keep those units stocked, perform terminal cleaning of patient rooms, and assist in passing meal trays and patient transport.(See accompanying position description.) This project will pilot the proposed role and evaluate the cost effectiveness and additional role definitions needed for full implementation.

Project Objectives:
1. Seek approval for job description and initial salary clearance.
2. Include unit staff in USA selection process.
3. Design and present USA training to those hired.
4. Implement the USA position.
5. Evaluate the position after six months.

Foreseen Problems/Issues and Plan to Resolve Them:
Staff must view this new role as essential for their operations in order for the position to be fully utilized. Reporting structures and supervision must be determined. This is yet another change for this unit's staff. Some may resist giving up previous activities. Staff input in selection of the USAs will assist in their integration into the unit. Evaluation parameters must be determined. See analysis plan.

Preferred Implementation Strategy(ies):
Pilot approach.
Enlist unit staff support.
Time analysis of role after 3 months.

People Factor: List people who should be involved in the project and how you plan to enlist them. What organizational structure is needed by the project?

Unit Practice Committee was involved in writing the job description. We will use this committee to plan the major components of the change.

Place Factor: What physical location, other department, or resources are needed for this project?

Previous clean utility room will now house supply exchange carts that USAs will use to distribute supplies to the nurse servers. They will use this space for supply ordering as well. Will use housekeeping closet for cleaning supplies.

Time Factor: Identify length of project, specific time needed for each phase. Complete tools as appropriate to project and attach.

The Gantt chart is attached. [See Figure 6.7.]

Communication Plan: Indicate all vehicles you plan to use to keep customers involved and informed of the project's progress.

Internal: Unit staff meetings will be used to inform all staff about the new role. Staff will volunteer for peer interview committee. Members will be drawn by lot. These staff will be trained in interview techniques. Staff feedback will be sought at two time intervals: 3 months and 6 months. Adjustments in the USA role will be determined after each evaluation.

External: Hospital newsletter will inform other employees of the pilot's progress on a quarterly basis.

Documentation Plan: List all forms of documentation needed to monitor progress of project. Include minutes, interim reports, and quality improvement documents.

1. Staff meeting minutes
2. Pre-mid-post surveys
3. USA orientation curriculum
4. Position descriptions
5. Interim report at 3 months
6. Final project report

Analysis Plan: What instruments are needed for analysis? What will the outcome criteria be, and how will they be measured?

1. The USA position description will serve as the basis of the staff pre-, mid-, and post-surveys. Detailed analysis will determine to what extent the staff support the position and what changes are deemed necessary.
2. A cost-benefit analysis will be performed with the assistance of Operations Research Department.

Cost Factor: Provide a budget for your project. Include pro forma, needs analysis, or cost-benefit analysis as appropriate.

Labor:	
1.4 FTEs of USA for six months	$ 9,000
150 project hours @$20.00/hr.	$ 3,000
Materials:	
2 Materials exchange carts	$ 1,400
20% increase in inventory to stock rooms	$12,000
Total costs:	$25,400
Costs/unit:	N/A

Sign-off:

Date: _____

Project Manager _____

Department Head _____

Administrator _____

FIGURE 5.7 Gantt Chart for Sample Project Plan

Activity	2	4	6	8	10	12	14	16	18	20	22	24	26
Plan approval	—												
Team/assignments	—	—											
Interview committee	—	—											
Interviews		—	—										
Hire USAs			—										
Write orientation curriculum	—	—	—	—									
Orientation			—										
USA implementation					—	—	—	—	—	—	—	—	—
Progress meetings	—			—		—		—			—		
Survey	—						—					—	
Data analysis		—					—						—
Time study				—									
Interim report due							—						
Final report												—	
Write newsletter update				—								—	

CHAPTER 7

> # Dynamics of Implementation

C areful planning for change lays the foundation that supports proper implementation and ultimate success. Pivotal to successful change is a well-designed and well-executed implementation strategy. The complexities of redesign require special attention to implementation since this type of change is often fundamental in nature.

LEADERSHIP SKILLS NEEDED

Leaders and their teams exact change. What are the leadership skills required to effectively implement redesign?

Vision and Alignment

The leader must have a vision for the redesign project and be able to communicate it effectively to the team. **Alignment** occurs when the team agrees with the vision and is committed to implementing the project. Without alignment, implementation may erode because key players do not share information, do not facilitate the redesign, or may even resist change.

Power, Influence, and Trust

The successful leader understands some basic principles about power, influence, and trust. **Power** comes from many sources. It is fundamentally a control over others that exacts a desired outcome due to implied or specified consequences. **Influence**, on the other hand, is a dynamic process; it seeks not to control but to set in place an interdependence that fosters cooperation (Carr, 1992). Power and influence can be conceived of as being on a continuum, from authority based to relationship based (Figure 7.1). The shades of authority-based power reside in institutionalized relationships. These flow from autocratic to democratic in nature and also from coercive to cooperative.

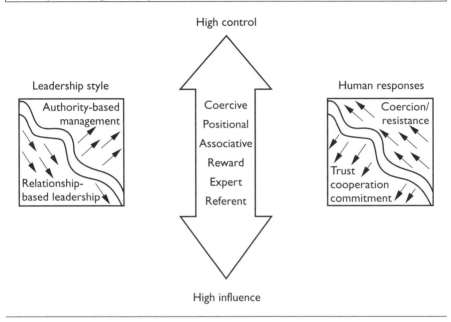

FIGURE 7.1 The Dynamics of Power, Influence, and Trust. This model shows the relationships of management style, trust, and the power-influence continuum.

On the relationship-based side, personal interactions and trust form the basis of the influence dynamic. These forms of influence are not coercive because they are derived from respect achieved over time due to either expert knowledge or personal relationships.

Institutional power does not produce commitment because coercion and commitment are mutually exclusive. Personal influence based on trust and respect may in fact foster commitment because coercion is not employed. Influence is mutual in that "you have the maximum opportunity to influence those whom you are willing to let influence you. This is just the reverse of power, which can be used effectively only by resisting others' power" (Carr, 1992, p. 135).

TIP

The stronger the power used, the greater is the resistance that can be anticipated.

Trust is fundamental to leadership. Without it, leaders can manage only because of institutional power. Leadership and mutual influence do not occur without trust. Trust may be won with consistency of purpose, open and direct communication, and principled behavior. Organizational mistrust can erode an individual's ability to build and maintain the trust of a team. If the organization does not require consistency of purpose, open and direct communication, and principled behavior, workers may not be willing to risk voicing and mutual influence (Kouzes & Posner, 1987) no matter what the leader does. (See "How to Create an Atmosphere of Trust.")

How to Create an Atmosphere of Trust

1. **Insist on open, honest, and direct communication.**
   - Confront passive-aggressive behavior immediately. It undermines morale.
   - Give as much information to the team as possible. People hate surprises.
   - Do not communicate through third parties. It sends the message that you do not care.
   - Eliminate blame. People will not risk innovation in an atmosphere that accommodates blame.
   - Set clear expectations. It fosters success in others.
   - Expose hidden agendas. They waste time and energy.
2. **Give feedback frequently. People need support and direction.**
   - Be free with praise. Ask yourself daily if you have given enough praise and recognition.
   - When correcting mistakes, offer specific, detailed ideas on how the behavior can be improved, including your standards for success. People cannot read your mind.
3. **Never take credit for others' work. It fosters resentment.**
4. **Walk the walk and talk the talk. Be a person of integrity.**
   - Operate from a philosophy. It is the only way your behavior can become consistent.
   - Strive for total consistency between your values and actions. It is the only way people can learn what to expect from you.
   - Support organizational values. If you cannot, think about changing organizations.
   - Always follow through on promises. It takes only one time for your credibility to be ruined and trust to be lost.

5. **Look for ways to demonstrate your trust in others. Trust is a two-way street.**
   - Think and talk positively about others. They will rise to your expectations.
   - Limit controlling others based on their abilities and past performance. It will foster autonomy.
   - Delegate. Allow the team the latitude to do it their way with reasonable independence.
6. **Allow yourself to be influenced by others. It is the only way you can influence them.**
   - Develop active listening skills. People need to know they were heard.
   - Relate to others as part of the team. Treat them with respect and as equals.
7. **Be an authentic person. This means sharing a part of yourself.**
   - Admit your errors. It shows you are human and can accept responsibility for your actions.
   - Relate with others on several levels. Some socializing will build team cohesion.
   - Let others know when you cannot take on a commitment and why. You do not have to own every problem.

Negotiation

Negotiating skills are essential for the effective project team. In the course of managing change, there are many opportunities for disagreement about substance or process issues. Fisher and Ury (1981) advocate what is known as principled negotiation: the parties negotiate from principles rather than positions. A variety of avenues for the resolution of problems can be used as long as guiding principles are addressed. The goal is reaching a mutually agreeable decision, a win-win approach.

On the other hand, once positions are stated, the parties feel compelled to defend their positions, making it more difficult to reach compromise or accommodation. The goal is achieving *your* position, a win-lose approach.

There are three characteristics of principled negotiation (Fisher & Ury, 1981, p. 5):

1. The agreement should be wise.
2. The process used to achieve agreement should be efficient.
3. The negotiation should be conducted in a way that preserves relationships for the future.

Delegation

Effective implementation of change requires leaders who can delegate appropriately and fully. **Delegation** is the "granting of authority to team members who share responsibility and accountability for task completion" (Decker & Sullivan, 1992, p. 579). Delegation extends work from what you can do to what you can influence. It is the initial act of management and leadership that requires artful implementation. Table 7.1 outlines the reasons that delegation is essential.

One aspect of successful delegation is the nature of the work itself. The work must be challenging in order to capture the spirit and zeal of the team. Carr (1992) defines three aspects of challenging work:

1. *Variety*, which may entail physical or mental changes from the routine. Team members have a chance to learn and test new skills.
2. *Completeness*, which refers to the connection the worker feels with the end product or customer. This connection fosters a sense of responsibility and ownership for the product. In the case of delegating, the worker feels in control of that piece that has been delegated and understands how it fits in the bigger picture.

TABLE 7.1 Benefits of Effective Delegation

CATEGORY	EFFECT
Work production	Increase productivity
	Improve time management
	Improve operations
Employee development	Expand employee skills
	Encourage creativity and initiative
	Increase employee value
Management development	Improve managers' leadership skills
	Improve communication
	Improve manager effectiveness
Employee relations	Build trust
	Improve employee participation and ownership of change
	Improve communication

3. *Problem solving*, which implies that workers feel empowered to solve problems they encounter in their work. It is important for teams, and individuals as well, to feel that their input into issues is valued and used. Valued contributions come from identifying and solving problems, not simply from normal production work.

Table 7.2 details the three key steps to effective delegation:

1. Assign responsibility.
2. Give authority and resources.
3. Establish accountability.

TABLE 7.2 Three Steps to Effective Delegation

STEPS	CONSIDERATIONS
1. Assign responsibility.	Select the best person for job based on:
	• Skills, knowledge, experience
	• Other assignments
	• Willingness to accept job
	Explain the task thoroughly:
	• Purpose, components of job
	• Time frame and desired outcomes
	Validate understanding, and answer questions about the assignment.
	• Put it in writing.
2. Give authority and resources.	Share knowledge needed for job.
	Inform others about the assignment and authority to do the job.
	Assign the resources to the delegated person.
	Let the delegated person control the processes to get the job done.
3. Establish accountability.	Set explicit deadlines.
	Set feedback intervals.
	Clarify criteria for success.
	Tie success to performance appraisal.

> **TIP**
>
> If people do not feel they control their work, they will not own the outcomes and may assume less accountability.

It is vital that the person who receives delegation be able to control the processes used to achieve desired outcomes. This does not mean absence of administrative support. Rather, the person is free to present a plan and to proceed in his or her own way. Sometimes approval will be needed, especially for critical processes. Ownership is vital in redesign where the knowledge worker is a fundamental element of the redesign process.

Time Management

Implementing redesign requires organization. Knowing what to do and when it must be done is essential. Creating planning time is an important first step for that to occur. The right tools also help in organization. Setting priorities will pay off in a smooth implementation phase. How do you sort out the vital from the trivial?

Figure 7.2 depicts four categories of activities, ranging from "must be done now and by you" to "fit it in later and perhaps delegate." By assigning all of your activities to a category, you can quickly determine what needs to be done first and what can safely wait. First, carefully consider if the activity

FIGURE 7.2 Time Management Categories. Four time management categories and their relationship to time and importance are depicted.

	Vital	Trivial
Urgent	A	C
Not time sensitive	B	D

A = Must be done now and by you.
B = May delay but must have plan to do. Can it be delegated?
C = Has to be done quickly. Is there time to delegate?
D = Fit it in later. Is delegation appropriate?

warrants being placed on the list. Frequently we are willing to take on activities that may more appropriately belong somewhere else. Form a habit of writing daily to-do lists based on the four categories.

Large tasks have to be broken down into more manageable steps, or they appear overwhelming. Project planning tools allow for the process of breaking work plans into more detailed activities. Their only limitation is a person's willingness to take the time to plan.

A final time management consideration is the leader's ability to eliminate extraneous activities in order to control the time needed to complete a project. Assignments may need to be adjusted in order to ensure success.

Decision Making

A **consensus** model of decision making is appropriate for incremental decisions where factors are known and the team is mature and prepared to participate in decision making. Allow group decision making only in areas the team has the authority to control. It is demoralizing for a team decision to be reversed because of political realities.

TEAMWORK

Individuals do not implement major change in a vacuum. Group work is essential to carry out complex initiatives. The dynamics and skills needed for true teamwork are discussed in the following sections.

Productive Meetings

Conducting a productive meeting is an important skill for a project manager. Team members should have the agenda far enough prior to a meeting so that they are prepared to work on the tasks at hand. It helps if the agenda is written in language that clearly states group objectives. Team members should understand their roles and any assignments ahead of time. Meetings should be planned at proper time intervals so that assignments may be carried out in the interim.

During the meeting, the leader's role is to move the agenda along. A proper balance of discussion and action is needed to allow the team to develop and also to get the job done. It may be necessary to draw the group back to the agenda if discussion strays for too long.

Minutes are an effective way to validate the work that took place and to assign future responsibilities. Figure 7.3 presents a useful minute format that clarifies action and responsible persons.

Figure 7.3 Meeting Minute Format

Date: _____

Committee: _____

Agenda Item	Discussion	Action	Responsibility	Date Due

Group Work

Team building is an important need for a new group. The leader can facilitate this by limiting competition among members. Activities that force members to work together for common goals benefit the group by emphasizing team over individual contributions. The team is further strengthened by involving them in decisions, using their ideas, and giving them credit for success.

Team learning must occur. By investing in human capital, the organization has a more highly functioning group. This may include many aspects of interpersonal skills or the technical information needed to perform a certain project. Techniques that help the team think in innovative ways are especially helpful because they allow the group to break away from their traditional approaches.

The project team becomes the major proponents of change. Their support helps to ensure smooth implementation (Waterman, 1991).

Self-Managed Teams

It takes a lot of development to have a team achieve the level of functioning needed to become a **self-managed team**—one that controls its own operations and outputs. It sets its own goals, identifies its measures of success, evaluates each other, and selects team members and the leader (Verespej, 1990). Teams pass through stages as they mature: from initiation, to team building, to alignment (Table 7.3).

The main benefits of using self-managed teams are improved quality, productivity, and morale. The main blocks to using these teams are listed in Table 7.4.

Feedback

Feedback is vital to a challenged workforce. People want to know that they are doing a good job and what it takes to succeed. Yet many leaders have trouble remembering to give feedback. Work actively at giving ongoing feedback.

TIP

One of the greatest challenges of leadership is to celebrate small successes so that they can build into larger ones.

TABLE 7.3 Stages of Team Growth

STAGE	CHARACTERISTICS	NEEDS
1. Initiation	Members are guarded	Establish trust
	Roles unclear	Form boundaries
	Tasks new	Clarify team goals
		Leader draws out members
2. Team building	Group roles established	Leadership helps members to develop
	Alliances form	Affiliation
	Conflict surfaces	Confrontation of unacceptable behaviors
		Negotiation/critical thinking skills develop
	Communication improves	Dialogue begins
3. Alignment	Major interpersonal issues resolved	Open, direct communication
		Natural leaders emerge
		Dialogue with increasing frequency
		More comfort with differences
	Group efforts focused on work	Productivity
		Group can set priorities
	Group shares values	Develop synergy

Negative feedback must be directed at the work, not the worker. Dialogue and direct communication are necessary to resolve issues. Dialogue does not occur without the leader's listening to the worker's side of the issue before a decision is made about the situation. Private, immediate problem resolution works best. A strong follow-through plan that monitors progress of the problem ensures behavioral change. The feedback must be useful to be helpful. It must be specific and detailed and be directed at problem resolution. Feedback should be customer focused. Table 7.5 identifies rules for giving effective feedback.

APPROACHES THAT WORK

When implementing redesign, there are many approaches that have proved effective. We examine some that work.

TABLE 7.4 Blocks to Using Self-Managed Teams

CATEGORY	REASON
Requires extensive worker training: Problem solving, coaching, communication, conflict management, team building	Costs of and commitment to training Lack of training resources Not valuing workers as resources Poor role models
Supervisory resistance	Job insecurity Reluctance to give up power Lack of collaborative skills
Little team authority: To select their leader	Leadership is based on hierarchy or assigned from above
To evaluate team members	Management controls evaluations
To control budget	Management controls budget
To set production goals	Management sets standards
Distrust	Management has not been consistent Information has been withheld Persons trying to undermine change
Team compensation model	Individual merit system in place Culture of individualism rather than team

Maintain Focus and Limit Scope

One of the enduring stories from Bill Clinton's 1992 presidential campaign was of the prominently displayed sign on the wall of campaign headquarters: "It's the economy, stupid!" Regardless of political ideology, a student of administrative theory appreciates the significance of boldly displaying the core vision to the troops. Change must be controlled and directed in order to achieve positive results that meet an ultimate vision. It is easy to get sidetracked. One of the main challenges of any change agent is how to focus activities toward desired outcomes. How to make the customer real to employees is a major challenge (Moss-Kanter, 1991).

Because events have a tendency to expand the project beyond original intentions, limiting project scope becomes an important technique. If the

TABLE 7.5 Rules for Giving Effective Feedback	
Be descriptive.	Give specific examples.
	State accurately without hyperbole.
	Concentrate on facts, not opinions.
Avoid labels.	Emotion-ladened adjectives place blame (e.g., "unprofessional" or "lazy").
Use good timing.	Do it in private.
	Assess the receiver's readiness.
	Allow emotions to settle first.
Set up dialogue.	Two-way communication is needed.
	Active listening is important.
Concentrate feedback.	Keep the issue clear.
	Don't cloud the issue with other data.
	Work on a plan for resolution.
Summarize decisions.	Repeat plan details.
	Set follow-up times.

leader allows the team to move in tangential directions to the real goal, an iceberg may become unearthed. These sidetracks must be controlled, or change becomes chaos. There is a distinction between limiting scope and limiting options needed to achieve redesign goals.

Project Coach

Having a senior person available as a resource to a project team can smooth change. The concept of coach is borrowed from athletics. A coach helps to move the team to a higher level of functioning and brings a dynamic to the equation that allows change to be everything it can be. The coach serves as a reflector who mediates events and experiences so the team develops new insights and is guided in unique directions.

Pilot Projects

A pilot project can be the best approach to take when initiating major change. The pilot unit becomes a laboratory for the dynamics of change in a more controlled environment than implementing change across the whole organization would allow.

> **TIP**
>
> Carefully choose the pilot unit so that the chances for success are maximized. Choose areas more accepting of change and ones where other changes have stabilized.

Limited Change and Broad Implementation

Another approach to change is to implement a more limited change project broadly across the organization. The benefit to this approach is that it standardizes systems across the organization. One example of such a change is to have the nursing staff on all units cross-trained to do phlebotomy. That approach allows the elimination of the centralized phlebotomy department so that the financial benefit of that change can be seen immediately. The political ramifications of such bold change are immediate. Besieged departments may muster their political chips in an effort to prevent loss of power. On the other hand, the change is more difficult to reverse when done completely across the organization because previous structures are not left in place to erode the change.

Foundational Strategies

Perhaps a future change is planned but several steps must be in place before the future can be realized. Such foundational changes set the stage for the real changes to come. For example, a move to a primary nursing model may simply be a foundational change to a later move to managed care. This tactic works well where staff behaviors must change or skills must be developed prior to the next step.

MANAGE CHANGE

The bottom line on redesign project implementation is managing change. (Refer to the dynamics of change discussed in Chapter 4.) Table 7.6 offers essentials for controlling change.

Steering Committee and Feedback to Team

The strategy of a carefully chosen steering committee in the redesign process is frequently used when change has political overtones because the committee may represent key power factions of the organization. The project plan

TABLE 7.6 Essentials of Controlling Change

STEPS	TECHNIQUES
1. Set standards.	Keep to specifications and time limits.
	Control costs.
	Set change control policy.
	Develop a communication plan.
2. Monitor benchmarks.	Use tools (e.g., Gantt and PERT charts).
	Watch resource use.
	Test as you go with inspection and auditing.
	Review progress reports.
	Revise the project as needed.
3. Correct variances.	Develop standards.
	Set strategies for compliance (e.g., incentives, controls).
	Make correction an ongoing effort.
4. Stabilize change.	Implement systems to support the change.
	Assign responsibility to maintain the change.
	Review the change at intervals.

can specify the points where decisions must be brought to the steering committee. (Review Figure 6.2.) This technique is especially helpful when the change is dynamic and many elements are unknown at the outset. The involvement of the steering committee molds the change on an ongoing basis.

Caution must be employed so that the steering committee functions at the intended level. Should its decisions concentrate only on policy, or will it need to be involved in operational issues?

Software Tools

There are many project management software programs on the market. Among them are Project Scheduler (Scitor Corp.), Microsoft Project for

Windows (Microsoft), and WorkMAN and WorkMAP (Reach Software). Most of these programs work by providing a framework for tracking project progress using computerized versions of the project management tools discussed in Chapter 6. Consult computer periodicals for up-to-date listings of such tools.

CLOSURE

Closure is necessary to complete a redesign project. The evaluation process may be one of the final aspects of a project. Evaluation of change is a broad topic and is discussed thoroughly in the next chapter.

Client Satisfaction

No redesign should be concluded without ensuring that the new processes have improved service to the client. Therefore, it is important to monitor client satisfaction before and after the change to determine its impact. To the extent possible, involving customers in the change process will enhance customer satisfaction.

Team Recognition

The team must be recognized as a whole. Individual contributions came together to produce the redesign effort. Carr (1992) writes, "A group of independents may make a beautiful constellation, but they make a lousy team" (p. 142). Rewards should be based on clear performance goals. The concept of equity should be used when rewarding teams.

A final act of the project may be a ceremony to release the team back to other duties. People who have worked together closely on a major project have created bonds. These can be recognized, and the team can experience closure for the project and a celebration of their accomplishments.

TIP

Establishing team recognition as an organizational standard helps to eliminate competition among team members.

MAINTAINING CHANGE

The responsibility for continuation, support, and maintenance of the change must find a permanent home. Many changes are not well maintained because at the end of implementation, it is assumed the change is final. It takes a period of time for changes to become permanent in peoples' minds. Systems must be in place to monitor the status of change and to assist in refinement of change as operating within the changed structure reveals need for modifications. The principles that guided the initial change must be kept in mind in order to prevent slippage.

SUMMARY

This chapter explored the dynamics of implementing change. A careful combination of leadership skills, teamwork, and approaches that work is needed to manage change on a large scale. Maintaining change cannot be taken for granted. Special attention to assigning responsibility for support and further development of the change ensures that redesign continues to evolve with the needs of the organization. Closure is necessary for the celebration of change and the team's accomplishments.

Evaluation of change from the perspective of the customer and the performance of the team will be discussed in detail in Chapter 8.

REFERENCES

Carr, C. (1992). *Team power.* Englewood Cliffs, NJ: Prentice-Hall.

Decker, P. J., & Sullivan, E. J. (1992). *Nursing administration: A micro/macro approach for effective nurse executives.* Norwalk, CT: Appleton & Lange.

Fisher, R., & Ury, W. (1981). *Getting to yes: Negotiating agreement without giving in.* Boston: Houghton Mifflin.

Kouzes, J. M., & Posner, B. Z. (1987). *The leadership challenge: How to get extraordinary things done in organizations.* San Francisco: Jossey-Bass.

Moss-Kanter, E. (1991, January–February). Even closer to the customer. *Harvard Business Review,* 9–10.

Verespej, M. A. (1990). When you put the team in charge. *Industry Week, 239*(23), 30–32.

Waterman, R. H. (1991, January 5). Adhocracy: Lessons from the change masters. *Hospitals, 65*(1), 56.

CHAPTER 8

Evaluation of Redesign

Quality, the core principle of redesign efforts, is often elusive to measure, but without evaluation, no one will ever know if the new initiatives are successful. J. Edwards Deming, the American who propelled Japan's quality movement, believed that with quality came a predictable degree of uniformity and dependability. In the auto industry, we think of it as zero defects. In health care, it is giving a uniform level of care and achieving uniform outcomes for all clients.

TWELVE KEY ASPECTS OF SUCCESSFUL QUALITY PROGRAMS

1. Management must be obsessed with quality.
2. There is a guiding system or ideology.
3. Quality is measured.
4. Quality is rewarded.
5. Everyone is trained in techniques for assessing quality.
6. Teams that cross barriers are used.
7. Small is beautiful.
8. There is constant stimulation to improve.
9. There is a structure for quality that parallels the organization's structure.
10. Everyone participates.
11. When quality improves, costs decrease.
12. Quality improvement is a never-ending journey. (Peters, 1987)

Requirements for Quality

There are ten steps to monitoring quality according to the Joint Commission on Accreditation of Healthcare Organizations (JCAHO, 1993):

1. Assign responsibility.
2. Delineate the scope of care and service.
3. Identify important aspects of care and service.
4. Identify indicators.
5. Establish thresholds for evaluation.
6. Collect and organize data.
7. Evaluate.
8. Take action.
9. Assess actions and document improvement.
10. Communicate relevant information.

Carrying out these ten steps is not enough, however. Evaluation must relate to relevant dimensions of performance according to JCAHO standards (1993). The dimensions of performance are:

1. "Doing the right thing," with respect to the efficacy and appropriateness of care, and
2. "Doing the right thing well," with respect to the availability, timeliness, effectiveness, continuity, safety, efficiency, and respect of care (JCAHO, 1993, p. 52).

Areas for Evaluation

There are three main areas for evaluation:

1. **Structure** evaluation monitors the "physical and organizational properties of the setting in which care is provided" (Donabedian, 1992, p. 357).
2. **Process** describes how care is provided and ways to improve systems and care delivery.
3. **Outcome** evaluation monitors results, both desired and undesired, that occur subsequent to care.

EXAMPLES OF EVALUATION COMPONENTS

- **Structure: The nursing unit has a master's-prepared nurse manager.**
- **Process: The team leader delegates to appropriate nursing staff after fully assessing patient needs.**
- **Outcome: Each patient will have a normal temperature at time of discharge.**

In order to achieve the level of evaluation needed to monitor and improve care, we must be clear from the onset as to what it is we wish to measure. This requires planning. The very act of planning evaluation can clarify issues, objectives, and measurement of outcomes.

EVALUATION PLANNING

Evaluation has to become part of the very act of doing business. It is not something that can be tacked on as an afterthought and still provide the needed information for constant improvement. An action research model (French, 1969) allows for evaluation to be an integral component of the change process. The steps in action research are:

1. problem identification
2. consultation
3. data gathering
4. diagnosis
5. client feedback
6. joint action planning
7. data gathering for rediagnosis

Decision making for continuous improvement is embedded in this model. Beginning evaluation prior to redesign is especially important in process evaluation, where the focus is on how change is implemented, and outcome evaluation, where pretest measures are needed to contrast with outcome data.

KEY REQUIREMENTS

The evaluation plan for collecting data must meet key requirements according to Schroeder (1994):

- It must have potential to generate or produce the needed data as part of the work itself.
- Standards of confidentiality and human rights must be met.
- Traits and culture of the group must fit the means of data collection.
- There is efficiency in regard to time, sample size, population, and resources.
- Data collection procedures create the least disruption to care.
- Collection formats are technically correct and can be analyzed appropriately.

Other key requirements that this author would add are:

- Data can be presented in a useful format and in a timely manner.
- Key people are trained to understand the evaluation system.
- Someone is in charge of evaluation and accountable to others for information flow.
- Managers are held accountable to improve practices based on evaluation measures.

FOCUS OF EVALUATION PLAN

Evaluation of redesign efforts focuses on four general areas:

1. organizational mission
2. general redesign principles
3. specific project goals
4. customer orientation to meet or exceed expectations every time

Organizational Mission

Each organization's mission is unique and should be one of the major guiding forces for change initiatives. Change should be consistent with organizational mission statements. Measuring achievement of mission is more challenging due to the broad statements that often characterize organizational missions. Mission can be further operationalized by identifying core values, strategic objectives, and other more measurable devices.

General Redesign Principles

Each organization should identify general guiding principles for its redesign efforts to ensure that all redesign efforts fit into a larger picture. Figure 8.1 highlights some principles that have been used to guide redesign planning in hospitals around the country. Evaluation must include measures of these principles whenever possible.

Specific Project Goals

Project goals should be written to stand the test of measurement. In other words, they should reflect concepts that are measurable. Unfortunately, often the tacit things in life are the most important. Given the tremendous complexity of the systems that redesign is attempting to change, it is often difficult to determine exact relationships between processes and outcomes. Contributing to measurement difficulty is the interaction of the multiple changes that occur within most redesign projects.

FIGURE 8.1 Redesign Principles

- Integration of systems and people
- Patient-focused approach
- Simplicity
- Efficient and effective
- Atmosphere for innovation
- Limit numbers of people patient must see
- Direct caregivers are cross-trained
- Multidisciplinary planning of change
- Shared decision making
- Process and outcome focus
- Changed people change systems
- Continuous improvement
- Evolving models
- Change is never finished
- Since models must meet patient needs, they may differ
- Open, honest communications

TIP

Every major step of a project should have a specified project goal.

Customer Orientation

No evaluation plan is complete without direct measurement of customer outcomes or satisfaction with care. Efforts to standardize process and outcome expectations are a core long-term goal of JCAHO and many managed care projects.

COMPONENTS OF EVALUATION

"Components of Evaluation" identifies the components that serve as the basis for obtaining evaluation data.

COMPONENTS OF EVALUATION

- **Practice standards**
- **Desired outcomes**
- **Organizational culture**
- **Benchmarks**
- **Quality improvement/quality assurance systems**
- **Project evaluation plans**
- **Performance appraisal systems**
- **Management by objectives goals**
- **Information systems**

EVALUATION TOOLS

Tools aid evaluators as they monitor data at every step of the evaluation process. Figure 8.2 identifies some typical evaluation tools used in identifying areas for improvement and monitoring processes and outcomes. Each type will be discussed. They may be used alone or in combination to produce the project evaluation plan.

FIGURE 8.2 Tools for Evaluating Redesign Efforts

Tools to identify areas needing improvement

    Brainstorming

    Flowcharts

    Focus groups

    Key informant

    Interviews

    Management rounds

    Monitors (audits)

    Pareto charts

    Surveys

Process monitoring tools

    Check sheets

    Fishbone diagram

    Flowcharts

    Focus groups

    Force field analysis

    Histograms

    Interviews

    Key informant

    Management rounds

    Monitors (audits)

    Nominal group techniques

    Pareto charts

Outcome monitoring tools

    Critical pathway monitor

    Focus groups

    Logs

    Management rounds

    Monitors (audits)

    Pareto charts

    Run charts

    Surveys

Brainstorming

The goal of brainstorming is to bring together people to identify new ideas about issues and answers. This is done in a nonjudgmental atmosphere where lists of possibilities are proposed without critique or discussion. The technique is equally successful with identifying problems, forging ideas about new ventures, or collecting data for strategic planning.

Brainstorming can involve an entire group or be used in break-out sessions to encourage smaller groups to tackle issues. The small group version sometimes allows for more ideas to be generated because participants tend to feel more comfortable than in larger groups. Brainstorming generally follows these steps:

1. Establish a recorder for each group. Writing all ideas on a flip chart allows for visual support of idea generation.
2. Review the ground rules for brainstorming:
   - All ideas are important.
   - All ideas are recorded.
   - No discussion or critique of ideas is allowed.
   - Stick to the topic.
3. Present the topic for discussion as specifically as possible. Allow for questions.
4. Have participants write down their own ideas first.
5. Brainstorm for a specified time or until no further ideas are generated.
6. Use this information in making changes.

Check Sheets

Check sheets monitor the number of times something occurs. The criteria for the event are listed in the left-hand column. In each succeeding column, checks are made each time the criteria is fulfilled within the specified time period. Figure 8.3 illustrates a check sheet format.

Critical Pathway Monitor

It is important to identify and monitor essential service delivery variables within established critical pathways. Which variables truly affect patient outcomes and should become central to pathway planning? Which ones are minor in their effect on outcomes? Valuable nursing and medical resources can be best utilized when there are answers to these questions for common clinical situations. Therefore, it is important to monitor the vital data that

FIGURE 8.3 Check Sheet Format

Reasons	January	February	March	April	May	June
Wrong patient	‖	‖‖		⎯	‖	‖
Wrong dose	⎯	‖‖	‖		⎯	⎯
Wrong drug	⎯	⎯	⎯	‖	⎯	
Wrong time		⎯	⎯	⎯		
Wrong route	‖		‖	⎯		⎯
Illegible order	⎯	⎯	⎯	⎯		⎯
Pharmacy error	‖‖	‖	‖	‖	‖	‖‖
Missed dose	‖‖‖	‖	‖	‖	‖	‖‖

pathway management affords. For example, length of stay can be used to compare variances among groups. What are the critical factors that separate "short stayers" from "long stayers"? Because these questions imply causal relationships, a statistical model is needed for this type of analysis and must be fitted to the type of data presented. (Statistical support is needed for such analysis. An in-depth discussion of statistics is beyond the scope of this book.)

Fishbone Diagram

A fishbone diagram is a tool to illustrate cause and effect. The main "bones" are usually determined by the type of setting. For example, Schroeder (1994, p. 36) cites generic categories for administrative issues: policies, procedures, people, and plant. These categories should be defined in a way that is useful for the purpose at hand. After the categories are determined, think of all the reasons that that category contributes to the problem. Schroeder (1994) cautions that listing symptoms or solutions is a frequent mistake. (A fishbone diagram is shown in Figure 5.9.)

Flowchart

Flowcharts are used to diagram actual or desired steps in a process: how things work. It is operationally very important to understand processes. A helpful approach to developing a formal flowchart is to use sticky labels to name steps. These can then be rearranged until the proper order and relationship of steps is identified. Key decision points are identified in the flowchart. Opportunities for errors, delays, or improvement are easily seen once the flowchart is documented. Figure 8.4 illustrates a typical flowchart before redesign and Figure 8.5 an improved process flowchart.

Focus Group

A **focus group** is a gathering of people who have been selected as representative of a certain customer base for the purpose of discussing key issues. This tool is used to identify areas needing improvement, to look at process issues, and to evaluate outcomes. Focus groups usually are conducted by experts in group dynamics who can keep the group focused on issues that have been predetermined. Another approach is more open to the focus group determining for itself the content of the discussion, typically when no data exist that can structure the evaluation.

FIGURE 8.4 Flowchart for Typical Process: Chest X-ray

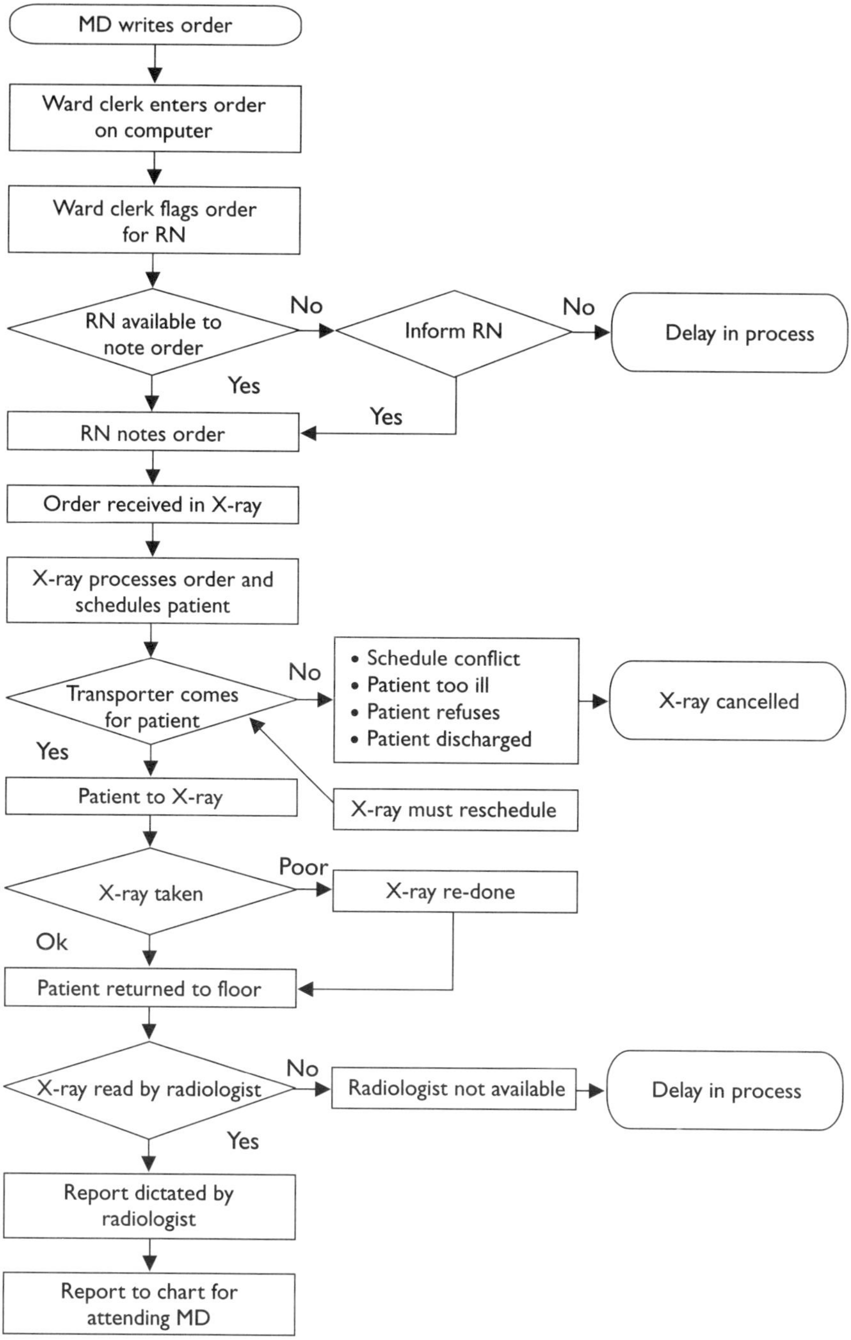

FIGURE 8.5 Flowchart for Improved Process: Chest X-ray

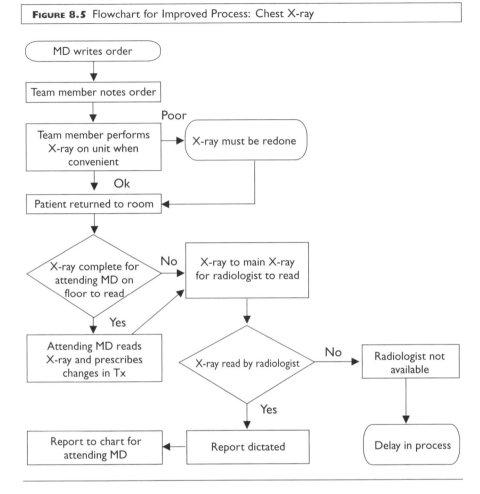

Patient focus groups can be conducted as a tool to identify areas of dissatisfaction or image problems—for example, delay in care, lack of responsiveness, or poor communication. Such groups may have important suggestions to improve processes from the customer perspective.

TIP

Focus groups serve as a forum for customers to express their needs or views. Listening is a vital skill for focus group leaders.

Staff focus groups are helpful when change is being considered. They may discuss work environment and quality-of-care issues. Specific work processes that take staff time away from patient care should be discussed. These groups often serve as a good starting point for small redesign efforts that can yield important results. Immediately observable improvements help to support the changes necessary for redesign to occur.

Data from focus groups must be retained. There are several ways to do this:

- A member can write key topics or comments on a flip chart.
- An audiotape or videotape can be used to capture all data. The audiotape can be transcribed so voices are not identified. Videotaping also captures nonverbal responses. Permission of all participants should be given prior to taping. It is important to note that some people may be less forthright with their comments if they are being taped.
- Trained observers can record comments about the group process as well as nonverbal and verbal data. This method may be perceived by the group participants as less threatening than taping, although recorder bias and interrater reliability issues may tarnish the data.

Force Field Analysis

Force field analysis is not new to those who are experienced in directing change efforts. This technique analyzes the direction and force of support for change (**driving forces**) and resistance to it (**restraining forces**). For change to succeed, the restraining forces must be weakened and the driving forces supported. It is possible to weigh the relative value of the forces using a numerical scale. The main benefit of this technique is to formalize the process of analyzing the change environment prior to setting strategies to secure support for change. Figure 8.6 shows a force field analysis. The anticipated response of important constituents to change is graphed on the vertical axis and can be tallied to quantify the support for or resistance to change.

Histogram

A histogram is a bar graph that measures a variation in process, such as length of stay for a category of patients. The data are often categorized or grouped to show relationships. (Schroeder, 1994). Figure 8.7 shows a histogram.

FIGURE 8.6 Force Field Analysis

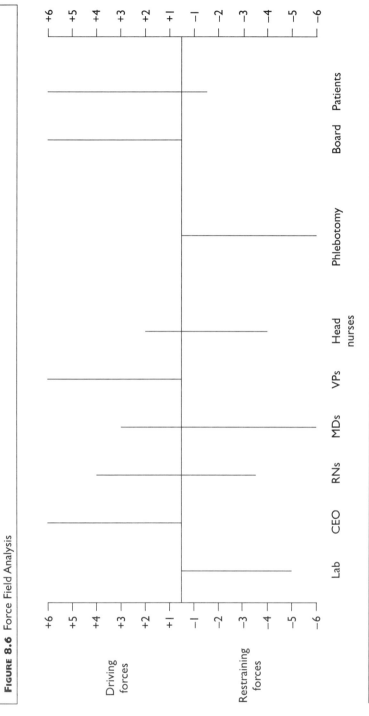

FIGURE 8.7 Histogram: Length of Stay for Open Heart Patients

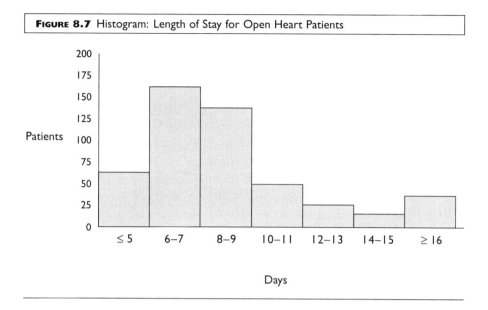

Key Informant

This technique involves interviewing or otherwise involving expert individuals who may contribute valuable perspectives on problem identification and program evaluation (Fitzgerald & Illback, 1993). Key informants do not take the place of focus groups, which give direct feedback on customer needs; rather, they add a professional perspective to broaden the decision-making base. This technique also addresses political issues related to change by determining how key informants feel about potential change.

Logs

This simple tool allows for periodic entry of data that are not expected to occur frequently or for problem-focused situations where the extent of the problem is unknown and must be monitored. Typical components of a log are date, time, item to be tracked, and reasons for occurrence. Figure 8.8 illustrates a log format.

Management Rounds

Management rounds are a key time to detect areas needing improvement, evaluate processes, and monitor outcomes. They are often conducted loosely and without a follow-up plan. In such a model, they are a social and political action, not a management function aimed at improving care.

FIGURE 8.8 Simple Log Format: Missing Unit-Dose Medications

Date	Time	Patient	Room	Medication	✓ if New Order

TIP

Remembering to give feedback about resolution of problems is an important aspect of management rounds.

As an evaluation and quality improvement action, management rounds can be broadly focused on whatever issues arise on each unit, or they may be targeted on specific functions across units. An example of a specific management round would be between the nursing manager and the housekeeping supervisor. They would predetermine the standards against which they were evaluating the cleanliness of nursing units. On less-structured rounds, the nursing vice president might discuss staff issues. The pocket-sized card in Figure 8.9 is helpful for documenting problems for later follow-up.

Monitors (Audits)

Monitoring aspects of care is a familiar activity for nurses. Monitors are used to identify areas needing improvement, evaluate processes, and examine outcomes. Monitors can employ simple check sheets or may use more complex forms. Critical to monitors is the identification of indicators and thresholds. (The quality improvement monitoring process was discussed in detail in Chapter 5, along with examples.)

Nominal Group Technique

A broad-based sample of people come together to generate ideas about issues and needs of common concern with a nominal group technique. It is a type of brainstorming session with a twist: each group member takes a turn at presenting his or her idea. This is a useful technique for groups whose participants may be reticent about speaking up due to lack of trust or consensus. Ideas are then condensed by consensus or voting to arrive at the best options. The rules for nominal group technique are otherwise similar to brainstorming.

Pareto Charts

Pareto charts help to clarify priorities by sorting out the "vital few" from the "trivial many" (Walton, 1986). Important aspects of care or opportunities for improvement can be categorized, and the leading causes or problems can be

---

Figure 8.9 Management Rounds Documentation Card

Unit: _____ Date: _____ Time: _____

Name	Issue	Recommendations	Action	Feedback

---

targeted for redesign, thus ensuring a maximum benefit from improvement efforts. The Pareto chart in Figure 8.10 relates to causes of patient falls. In this example, interventions for patient falls would concentrate on reducing confusion and medication-related falls while educating staff regarding safety actions. Histograms differ from Pareto charts by depicting a process rather than examining causes of a problem for the purpose of targeting interventions.

Run Charts and Control Charts

Run charting reflects data frequency over time for the purpose of trending. It is a visual representation of the data in graph form. The horizontal axis represents time measures and the vertical axis the trend of the variable of

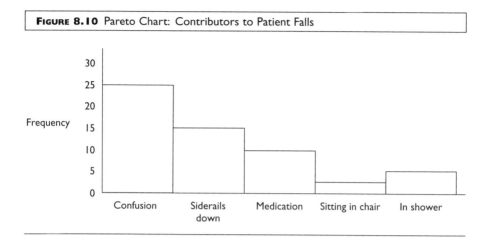

FIGURE 8.10 Pareto Chart: Contributors to Patient Falls

interest. Lines connect the points of time. Means, medians, or midpoints often are plotted as well for easy comparison.

In control charts, normal ranges for high and low are represented by lines against which the data can be compared visually. Figure 8.11 shows a control chart.

Surveys

Surveys are a means to evaluate the satisfaction of patients and associates regarding specified topics. They also are used to rate "dimensions such as intensity, duration, and/or severity of the variable(s) of concern" (Fitzgerald & Illback, 1993, p. 407).

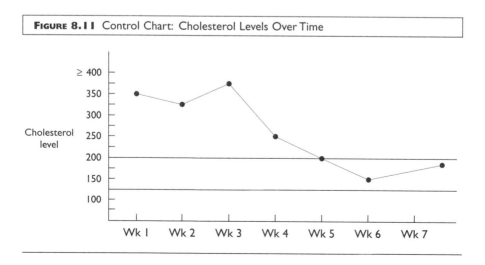

FIGURE 8.11 Control Chart: Cholesterol Levels Over Time

Surveys need to be constructed properly so that questions do not bias responses. For example, the following question would tend to bias responses against 12-hour shifts:

Which statements are true about 12-hour shifts?
(A) They are too long and tiring.
(B) There is lack of continuity of care across the week.
(C) There is poor communication with other staff due to working fewer days.
(D) Those who work fewer days have a better personal life.

The following wording is better:

Which shift length would you prefer?
(A) 8 hours
(B) 10 hours
(C) 12 hours

TIP

A direct contact approach in handing out surveys often results in better participation.

How surveys are conducted affects the reliability of results. Having a neutral party conduct the survey and ensuring confidentiality of responses will improve return rates and honesty of responses. Respondents must understand the importance of the survey and how the information will be used before they will be motivated to participate.

SUMMARY

All redesign efforts are undertaken in an effort to improve processes and to improve the quality of the product: patient care. More consistency and predictability in both processes and outcomes should result from quality improvement and redesign initiatives. Evaluation must be integrated into the entire redesign planning process to ensure these results. Measurable results support redesign by proving outcomes are met and objectives achieved.

These can be especially important when there are political enemies of redesign. This chapter presents evaluation tools and strategies for successfully measuring these outcomes.

REFERENCES

Donabedian, A. (1992). The role of outcomes in quality assessment and assurance. *Quality Review Bulletin, 18*(11), 356–360.

Fitzgerald, E., & Illback, R. J. (1993). Program planning and evaluation: Principles and procedures for nurse managers. *Orthopaedic Nursing, 12*(5), 39–44.

French, W. L. (1969). Organization development: Objectives, assumptions and strategies. *California Management Review, 12*(2), 23–34.

JCAHO. (1993). *The Joint Commission Accreditation Manual for Hospitals, 1994.* Oakbrook Terrace, IL: JCAHO.

Peters, T. (1987). *Thriving on chaos: Handbook for management revolution.* New York: Harper & Row.

Schroeder, P. (1994). *Improving quality and performance: Concepts, programs and techniques.* St. Louis: Mosby.

Walton, M. (1986). *The Deming management method.* New York: Perigee Books.

CHAPTER 9

Organizational Development

JUDE A. MAGERS

Day-to-day **organizational development** (OD) work by nurse executives is an art at the core of successful redesign of the nursing organization. It is an artful discipline necessary to facilitate alignment of an organization's vision, mission, objectives, core processes, and desired outcomes. OD is fundamental work for all leaders at every level of the organization. It requires skills that facilitate growth in the human side of the work. OD alignment work is based on six core skills:

1. **Integrative structuring** process work
2. **Cultural listening**
3. **System thinking** for whole system change
4. Self-reflection in a climate of ambiguity
5. Team building
6. Group work

The ethics of practice of the leader, aware of her or his role in OD work, is guided by trust in the individual and in group process, honest dialogue, confidentiality, respect for the person and group, recognition of the history of the organization, reflective thought, and a belief in possibilities. The action plans of the OD leader are based on these core skills and ethics of practice.

ILLUSTRATING CORE SKILLS THROUGH ACTION PLANS

The leader's action plans in OD are expansive and in constant evolution. This section explores the six core skills through action plans used to facilitate redesign work.

Integrative Structuring Process Action Plan

Traditional organizations are flattening, core processes are replacing departmental structures, and information systems are integrating for "just in time" access and input. Today's successful leader must build an interdependent infrastructure of relationships spanning traditional boundaries of authority and functions. Integrative structuring process is a skill that is practiced daily as the leader strategically questions basic assumptions. (See "Action Steps for Integrative Structuring.")

ACTION STEPS FOR INTEGRATIVE STRUCTURING

- **Do we know where we are going? (vision)**
- **Do we have the right people involved to get there?**
- **Do we have the right database to support our work?**
- **Do we know our customers?**
- **Do we know what our customers want?**
- **Do we know our key partnerships in decision making?**

> **TIP**
>
> Vision: You need to know where you are going in order to get there.

The leader challenges work groups to answer these questions and helps members become aware of the interdependency essential for success in redesign. Turf issues and departmental politics must be erased for optimum integration.

Cultural Listening Action Plan

Leader must understand that culture is at the heart of every change process. Culture is present within all groups and is demonstrated in artifacts: rituals, symbolic gestures, symbols, language, and thought processes (Figure 9.1). Culture is carried and transmitted by individuals. It is developed and learned as individuals live and work together.

FIGURE 9.1 Examples of Culture

Symbol	Ritual	Sign
Uniforms	Wearing a stethoscope	Notes on the report door
Name tag	RN shift report	Staying with the patient
Journals	Shared decision making	Clocking in by machine
Gifts	Calling the patient's home	Touching the patient
Coffee cup	Celebrating successes	Consulting with a colleague

Basic assumptions are unconscious and are brought to consciousness as an individual or group's symbols, rituals, signs are explored. We refer to these "visual aids" as artifacts.

One of the key responsibilities of the leader is to articulate and help clarify the organizational vision. Vision work requires cultural listening. Cultural listening is an action plan for the leader because it helps the leader to understand the existing reality for members of the organization in relation to the desired vision. **Reality** may be culturally at odds with the vision.

TIP

Culture is at the heart of change.

Culture is built on the assumptions and beliefs that lie below the consciousness of most members. Through cultural listening, assumptions and beliefs are brought to the awareness of the organization's members. This gives them power to identify new assumptions and beliefs that will move them toward the desired future. Without this work, an organization remains fixated on the present and has little or no energy to support needed change. "Action Steps in Cultural Listening Exercise" sets out a simple but powerful cultural listening action plan to uncover cultural assumptions and beliefs and create energy among a group's members to move toward a common vision.

ACTION STEPS IN CULTURAL LISTENING EXERCISE

1. **List the seven most important values in your work.**
2. **Prioritize the values.**
3. **Separate out the top three.**

4. **How do you express or demonstrate these top three values in your day-to-day work? List rituals, symbols, language, and ways of thinking.**

5. **What keeps you from expressing values you believe in?**

6. **If you could change your work to express your values, what would it look like? (Describe in detail.)**

7. **Given the vision of the organization, what relationship is there to individual values and their expression and the desired future? Conflict? Alignment? Connected?**

8. **Spend 20 minutes of quiet time to consider what new insights you have about the data provided by the individual or group.**

9. **Report out. Talk about the reflective time. What happened for the participant(s)? Did the participant(s) identify a need for change? Is there awareness of new rituals, behaviors, or ways of doing things? Is the conflict too great between values and vision?**

The leader desires to understand the members and their reality and to help the members articulate their relationship and roles to the vision. There are no right or wrong answers in this action plan and its steps. It is a process designed to encourage open expression so that the leader and members can identify common ground essential for system thinking and change.

System Thinking for Whole System Change Action Plan

The leader of a redesign process recognizes the complexities inherent in change. Transforming a system is a very difficult challenge to even the most skilled leaders. Having spoken of the power of culture and the need to attend to the sacred cows of ritual, language, and symbols, the leader must approach system change with system thinking. It is helpful to look at this action plan from a perspective of eight functions involved in system thinking and change (Figure 9.2):

1. Define the scope and boundaries of the system identified for change. The change process begins with this functional step.
    *   Interview leaders individually, asking, for example:
        What has happened to suggest a system change is needed?
        What system(s) do you specifically see as needing change?
        Who do you see as key people in helping the change to occur?
        What is off-limits in conducting system change?

Figure 9.2 Functions Involved in System Thinking and Change

1. Define the scope and boundaries of the system identified for change. The change process begins with this functional step

2. Assess the needs and goals of the identified system for change.

3. Diagnose the system for points of inertia. Points of inertia may be identified as a process, structure, or person. These points are commonly unconscious in the day-to-day operations of a system.

4. Identify focuses of control by the providers of care who are involved in the system change process. This is usually formal and informal. Both must be known for successful change.

5. Identify communication processes that are used by the system for change.

6. Restate the scope and boundaries after collection of data from steps 1–5. Use a broad representative group that includes customers, providers, formal leaders, informal leaders, stakeholders, and suppliers to the system.

7. Contract with the established leadership and key stakeholders responsible for initiating the change process. This is the development of a formal charter and is an important ritual for change.

8. Implement the interventions for whole system change.

What is the desired decision-making process for approving change recommendations?

What financial resources are available for a system change?

These questions elicit responses that will be useful in planning interventions.

- Build consensus by bringing the leaders together after the individual interviews. Work with the group to arrive at consensus on scope and boundaries. Use data gathered from interviews to structure boundaries and scope. Keep a cultural listening stance during this work. Look for themes in the dialogue and control areas. Notice who speaks, and about what issues. Notice who does not speak, and be sure to check on this person's position in defining scope and boundaries.

2. Assess the needs and goals of the identified system for change.

- Conduct a survey of the system's customers. Based on the size of the system, a survey may be conducted with a statistically representative number of the customers. Key questions to ask in a survey are these:

What do you believe needs to change?

If you could have this system in any form, what would you want to see?

What do you most value in a desired system?

What do you most value in the current system?

- Review any evaluative data collected within the system relevant to the identified area of change. Look for themes that relate to strengths and weaknesses, decision-making models, and regulatory requirements.

3. Diagnose the system for points of inertia—processes, structures, or people. These points are commonly unconscious in the day-to-day operations of a system.

   - Cultural listening is required to notice the use of language and decision-making patterns that may reveal a great deal about sources of inertia—for example: "they-we," "we can't do that," "it was tried before and did not work," "that is part of our culture," "we will need top management to make a decision," "the hospital said we could not do this," and "we have a policy that prevents us from doing this."
   - Ask the customers and service providers what they believe are the main obstacles to a successful system change.

4. Identify focuses of control by the providers of care who are involved in the system change process. The focuses are both formal and informal. Both must be known for successful change.

   - Ask the members of the system identified for change, "who makes the decisions that have an impact on the system?"
   - Identify the informal leaders in the system by culturally listening to where members go for help, support, and decisions. Notice who is referenced for as needed in a change decision.

5. Identify communication processes that are used by the system for change.

   - Request formal members of the communication system to participate directly in the change work.
   - Clearly identify the means to access communication processes and instruments to ensure timely and supported communication efforts.
   - Use time lines, and identify members responsible for ensuring communications within the system of change and external to the system. Request routine reports. Provide more, not less, structure for communication if the system has a high level of mistrust among its members.

6. Restate the scope and boundaries after collection of data from the previous functional steps. Use a broad representative group that includes customers, providers, formal leaders, informal leaders, stakeholders, and suppliers to the system.
   - Develop a vision statement using a broad-based membership from within the identified system as well as the customer base. The vision needs to be written after reviewing the data gathered from the previous functional steps.
   - Restate the scope and boundaries, objectives of change, expected outcomes, and time line for the change proposal. This step is critical to ensuring alignment among the leadership and members of the system in need of change.

7. Contract with the established leadership and key stakeholders responsible for initiating the change process. This development of a formal **charter** is an important ritual for change. The work is led by the system change leader, but a cross-representation of the membership of the system for change participates in authoring the charter.
   - The leader responsible for conducting the previous functional steps ensures preparation of a formal charter statement with the following elements:
     The purpose for the whole system change
     The vision for the system
     The identified scope, boundaries, and objectives
     Time line
     Budget
     Plan for anticipated interventions
   - The leader and members present the charter to the leadership and key stakeholders for agreement and signatures.
   - The leader and members of the authoring group present the charter to the total membership of the system for change.

8. Implementation of interventions for whole system change occurs after the previous seven steps are completed. The change process continues with this step but becomes more visible among more members as interventions focus on the processes that have an impact on the total membership within the system and those external to the system.
   - Interventions must be custom designed for the system. The interventions are determined in part by:
     Cultural norms and learnings
     Level of change initiative (Table 9.1)

TABLE 9.1 Levels of Whole System Change	
LEVELS	**EXAMPLES**
Micro	Job description analysis and development
	Time management
	Team development
	Role clarification
Macro	Departmental vertical and horizontal integration
	Service line development
	Functional mergers
	Shared governance
	Acute to primary health care system
	Leadership turnover
Global	Institutional mergers
	Provincial to national system integration
	National to international trade network
	Regional to international telecommunication network
	Health care reform
	Local to international information highway

Time lines

Urgency

Financial support

Readiness of the group involved in change

Skill level of the group members involved in change

- Interventions must be responsive to the vision, objectives, time line, and desired outcomes identified in the charter.

"System Change Interventions" shows the complexity of this process.

SYSTEM CHANGE INTERVENTIONS

- **Project management**
- **Work flow**
- **Team development**

- Facilitation of decision making
- Work skill analysis and design
- Career development
- Role clarification
- Mission and vision development
- Cultural listening
- Cultural assessment
- Empowering processes
- Cross-training
- Group process
- Education to change process
- Continuous quality improvement
- Change conference
- Open space conference

There are several levels at which system change occurs. Table 9.1 gives examples of three levels: micro, macro, and global.

The intensity of a redesign process employing system thinking requires that the leader be reflective. This is especially important in the midst of continuing ambiguity typical of the redesign environment.

Self-Reflection in a Climate of Ambiguity Action Plan

The leader of a redesign change process must be reflective, not reactive. Today's change processes are constant. The leader must be flexible in this reflective stance and not need to see the world in absolutes. The scope of possibilities is endless in the midst of ambiguity. Creativity is limited if the leader responds in a rigid way. The members need to see assurance in the leader in the midst of ambiguity. The steps in this process are simple and daring, and they require reflective thought. (See "Action Steps in Self-Reflection.")

ACTION STEPS IN SELF-REFLECTION

- Set a vision that has enough clarity to lead the group.
- Exchange vision ideas with the membership.
- Demonstrate consistent behavior that reflects the vision.
- Respect people even if there is conflict and disagreement.
- Recognize your limitations, and set time for reflection.

The reflective leader will continue to be challenged as the value for individualism becomes less acknowledged and the need for teamwork becomes more the norm in many redesign efforts. Along with the action plans comes a critical skill in team building.

Team Building Action Plan

Leaders in redesign efforts frequently identify the need for team building, although a team is not the answer for every redesign effort or every work group need. When teamwork is identified as central to a redesign effort, leaders must model and encourage others to participate in its development. For members of a change process asked to work in teams, there is much team development work to be done:

- vision development and clarity
- goal clarity
- communication and ground rules for the group
- contracting in needed degrees of confidentiality
- determining **work style preferences** (McFletcher Corporation, 1979)

See "Action Steps for Team Building" for one approach. In this approach, each member completes questions to be shared with members of a newly formed group. The member shares only what is comfortable. This is repeated after 3 months of working together as a formal team.

ACTION STEPS FOR TEAM BUILDING

- **What do I bring to this work that respects my talents and strengths?**
- **What do I need in a group to feel satisfied that my work is meaningful?**
- **What causes me not to participate in a group?**
- **What helps me participate in a group?**
- **My best life experience as a team member was ... [describe elements that made it the best].**

Inherent in team development is much investment in group process work. It is not necessary for all work groups to act as teams, especially when their work is of short duration and if their work deploys them to diverse settings. If a group is identified to help in a change design project and does not identify itself as a team but as a work group, then the expectations are different, and a different skill is required by the leader in the design process.

Group Work Action Plan

Some work by its very nature is best done by members identified as a work group. A work group has traits that may appear similar to a team but are actually lived out in the work setting in a different manner, and the leader needs to attend to these members in a different manner. The members may originate from the same department, but the focus of their work is responsive to customer needs and not internally focused to a common content of work. This is common in work redesign because of the potential variety of customer groups, supplier groups, and multiple entries into the system. The leader focuses on individual goals and objectives, individual time lines for work completion, and providing resources as members identify needs. Common needs of work groups are illustrated in "Action Steps for Work Groups."

ACTION STEPS FOR WORK GROUPS

1. **Clarify the purpose of the group and the difference from a team.**
2. **Bring the members together periodically to share the focus of their work.**
3. **Celebrate any breakthroughs that members may have in the redesign work, and share them with the group.**
4. **Ask members to provide educational experiences to the members that have been obtained from knowledge acquired in the redesign work.**

The work of a group can be powerful if the members stay focused on customer needs. A work group's major weakness occurs when its members lose sight of the customer and become critical of each others' work. Thus, the leader must lead the work group using the action steps stated.

SUMMARY

The work of leaders in organizational development is constant in today's environment. It is multidimensional and dynamic. As long as we have organizations, there will be inquiry into the how and why of change in these complicated structures. The shift toward greater accountability by all members of an organization mandates that the leader focus on the needs of its members to develop skills in information systems, decision-making models, competency structures, and focus on customer service as a driving core value.

This is a new world and specifically new for the nursing organization. This is no longer a world to be controlled from the top but to be owned, created, and determined by its full membership. This can be done only by developing methodologies that involve the workers, who must adapt to this new work environment. Thus, the leader's work in organizational development is to:

- ask the questions.
- give few prescriptive answers.
- set a clear vision.
- explore the perceptions of the members.
- help the staff to identify the core values that bring meaning to the workplace.

This is the leader who is key in supporting creative thought and action in redesign work that positions an organization for success.

REFERENCES

Anderson, B. (1993). *Empowering leadership.* Whitehouse, OH: Innovative Systems.

Block, P., Petrella, A., & Weisbord, M. R. (1992). *Improving whole systems: A briefing.* Plainfield, NJ: Block, Petrella & Weisbord.

McFletcher Corporation (1979).

Nadler, D. A., Gerstein, M. S., Shaw, R. B., & Associates. (1992). *Organizational architecture: Designs for changing organizations.* San Francisco: Jossey-Bass.

Schein, E. H. (1985). *Organizational culture and leadership.* San Fransico: Jossey-Bass.

Senge, P. M. (1990). *The fifth discipline.* Garden City, NY: Doubleday Currency.

Senge, P. M. (1974). *Thomas-Kilmann conflict mode instrument.* Tuxedo, NY: Xicom, Incorporated.

Wisbord, M. R. (1992). *Discovering common ground.* San Francisco: Berrett-Koehler.

Wheatley, M. J. (1992). *Leadership and the new science: Learning about organization from an orderly universe.* San Francisco: Berrett-Koehler.

Wheatley, M. J. (1979). *Workstyle preference inventory.* Scottsdale, AZ: McFletcher Corporation.

CHAPTER 10

Continuous Change: One Future Generation Redesign Model

Redesign is never complete. By the very nature of continuous improvement philosophy, further alterations in products and processes always will be forthcoming. This is perhaps the hardest concept to impart to associates who feel bombarded with change.

Many people resist change because they think it implies that what they had been doing in the past was not valued or appreciated. For this reason, it is vital that redesign and other continuous improvement efforts be directed by the affected work groups.

Many old-line managers may not be comfortable with the concept of trusting the process and may not want to relinquish control. Some believe, foolishly, that change can be mandated and be lasting. People will always gravitate back to comfortable behavior, especially when the new behaviors are not properly understood or supported. Therefore, people must understand the value of change. We know there are resisters to every change. Time often has a way of sorting that out. But if a critical mass of people is not brought on board, the change will fail outright.

This chapter presents one model of redesign. How that model has evolved over a five-year period is illustrative of what continuous redesign means.

INITIAL REDESIGN MODEL

Redesign is based on a patient-focused philosophy, so the efforts at St. Vincent's Health Services in Indianapolis have been directed toward simplifying and bringing services closer to the patient. This focus has led to a decentralized care delivery system based on needs analyses for each specific patient population.

The need to go through the redesign process afresh with each unit that enters patient-focused care quickly became apparent. Needs vary by types of patients and by physician and clinician practices. Those closest to the services are the experts who understand the patient care process.

The first unit to undergo this process was a general surgical unit in 1989. It was done from the top down because of the need to understand the redesign process and because of the risks associated with an initial venture. However, associates were asked to volunteer for this prototype unit, and their input was sought in a limited way in planning for unit needs.

Extensive patient analysis showed that laboratory tests such as electrolytes, blood urea nitrogen, creatinine, blood sugars, urinalysis, complete blood count, protime, and partial prothrombin time were common. The 80/20 rule guided the selection of these tests: approximately 20 percent of the tests represented 80 percent of the volume (O'Day & Fisher, 1994). A satellite lab was placed on the unit, and initially all staff were trained to run tests and to perform quality control checks on the equipment. It has since become apparent that there is no need to train all people in this area. It is expensive, and they must perform this service frequently to maintain their competency. Now a core lab group is maintained and scheduled to cover unit needs.

Since many surgical patients require flat plate x-rays, an x-ray room was placed on the floor as well. It did not take long to realize that Indiana radiology licensing law was not going to support cross-training for this service. Some of the technicians who entered the floor for cross-training to patient care were already certified in radiology, so they were the only ones who could perform this service on the unit. Today, this service is underutilized and has not been replicated on subsequent units.

TIP

Be well versed in state licensing issues prior to implementing specialty training.

Teams of RNs, LPNs, and technicians were established. Everyone on the team had the title "Team Care Specialist" and their discipline (RN, LPN, or technician) on their name tags. Everyone was to be cross-trained to perform all services so that patients would not have multiple people attending to their needs. The concept of dealing with each need as it arises and not having to pass an activity off to someone else was followed where possible. Of course, there are activities that are uniquely the function of the RN, and those have not changed.

Cross-training included phlebotomy and respiratory services such as oxygen setups, incentive spirometry, postural drainage, percussions, aerosols, acetylcysteine, and albuterol sulfate treatments. The technicians also were trained in basic data collection for patient status, patient care, and nonsterile treatments. All team members were educated about team concepts, delegation, conflict management, and communication. Shared decision-making councils with all levels of associates were initiated to set floor policy regarding peer relations, laboratory core issues, quality improvement, and education.

A satellite pharmacy was placed on the floor, and the patient rooms and the physical core of the unit were renovated. Many previously central unit functions are now performed in the rooms. Each room has a nurse server with individual patient medication spaces, a charting area, and drawers for supplies that are needed for surgical patients. Initially, the patient charts were placed in the rooms, and computer terminals were in each room for order entry by the team with hopes for computerized nurse charting in the near future. There no longer was a central nursing station. In its place were several substations that were physically close to the patient rooms of each team. But nurses were rarely in the substations; rather, they were most often in the patient rooms. This aspect of redesign still is true today.

After six months of operation, initial evaluation showed increased patient, physician, and staff satisfaction with the unit. Staff retention was near 100 percent, and patient length of stay was reduced.

There were some communication problems for physicians presented by this model. They no longer had a charge nurse to answer all their questions and had to find each patient's nurse. This was good from a collaboration standpoint but not from a physician time perspective.

Several creative approaches to resolve communication problems have been used. A team board placed in the hall beside each nursing substation lists the nurses' names and assignments for the shift, so doctors can see which nurse is working. A list of telephone numbers for each substation, along with the rooms for that station, is provided to the physicians so they can call directly to that area. The next problem to be addressed was that nurses were rarely in the substations to answer telephones because they were in patient rooms. A solution that several units now use is cellular telephones that the RNs carry. Only physicians are given these numbers. The cellular telephones reduce the number of times that nurses must run to the substation telephone and reduce the time physicians spend waiting for telephones to be answered. The nurse still may need to go to the substation to check something for the doctor.

This unit is a pacesetter and innovator to this day. It initiated a new documentation system based on exception charting (ex: assessments using a coded flowchart where only abnormals must be explained) and problem-oriented record in 1993, and it was early to use critical pathways. This unit then piloted a computerized nurse charting system that runs exclusively on critical pathways. The staff are active in shared decision making for the unit. They control their own quality improvement program, competency training, and peer review processes. Innovation is a unit culture and staff expectation.

FUTURE GENERATION MODELS

Subsequent patient-focused care units have learned from the surgical unit's experiences. Each unit has enlisted the help of experts from previous redesign units to serve as advisers to their processes. Each process has become more decentralized. The second units to move to patient-focused care were led by systems people with the unit managers participating. Now, unit managers and their staff direct redesign with broad participation from all customers and support from systems people. This is possible because of the growth of shared decision making. Staff now are able to lead subgroups and accomplish change with minimal direction.

LESSONS LEARNED

The organization's culture must be assessed, and plans for its transformation to support redesign must be foundational to change. The role of organizational development experts in this process has proved vital for resolving tough issues in volatile areas.

A clear, shared vision that is communicated with enthusiasm and commitment is vital (O'Day & Fisher, 1994). Agreement on principles of redesign clarifies objectives and supports an underlying structure without limiting innovation and creativity. Trust is vital as well, for without it, there is no empowering environment to support the needed risk taking associated with innovation.

TIP

Needs for each unit vary due to differences in physician practices and patient needs.

Each change builds on the system in place and continues to make improvements and refinements. Cross-training is unit specific. Worker transferability and staffing flexibility become issues due to this specificity. Fully cross-trained float RNs who are flexible and strong in their skills are a valuable resource and are appropriately compensated.

Political tensions may continue from centralized service departments whose roles have eroded with the progress of patient-focused care. This may be true of physician groups as well. The best way to deal with these realities is to enlist these people into the change process and to make them negotiate with peers from a patient perspective. Compromise is possible within the framework of redesign principles.

Celebration is essential. Not only must the victories be celebrated, but less successful changes must be applauded for their effort and then used as a basis for trying once again. For example, the postcardiac surgical units have maintained a resource nurse, primarily to facilitate physician needs, assist teams, and coordinate patient transfers and lab results reporting.

SUMMARY

Redesign is one form of continuous improvement of nursing systems. It is popular because the inefficiencies of current systems can no longer be tolerated in today's health care environment.

Our institutions have not been patient focused. They have evolved around revenue-generating departments. In the reality of diagnosis-related groups and capitation, many of these departments no longer generate revenue and, in fact, raise costs. Health care must do what other industries have had to do to survive global competition: find the most effective and efficient way to provide services. That may mean redesign of existing systems. More important, it may mean redefining business to cover an entire continuum of care services for capitated customers. This shift of thinking is as fundamental as the paradigm shifts of redesign and innovation.

Nurses are essential for patient care and must be prepared to be full players in these dynamic times. Armed with the skills to lead nursing redesign for the future, they can protect patients' interests while ensuring a viable and vital role for nursing.

REFERENCE

O'Day, L., & Fisher, M. L. (1994). Third generation redesign: Lessons from the field. In D. L. Flarey (Ed.), *Redesigning nurse care delivery: Transforming our future*. Philadelphia: J. B. Lippincott.

GLOSSARY

As we embark on a new frontier, our terminology often changes to reflect new realities. These terms are defined here in an effort to help the reader understand basic concepts upon which redesign is built.

Action Practice must be consistent with content themes in order for cultural synergy to occur.

Aggregate project planning A technique that looks at all levels of projects for all departments of an organization with the intent to coordinate and control change.

Alignment Individuals have collective agreement and commitment to a goal.

Artifacts The rituals and stories that support cultural symbols by making culture visible, audible, and tangible to an individual or group.

Aspect of care In quality improvement terms, any activity or part of care that may potentially affect patient outcomes. The next step after identifying aspects of care is to create indicators to measure attainment of the aspect of care.

Benchmarking A desirable standard (the best demonstrated practice) against which to measure performance and target goals for improvement.

Break-even analysis The minimum volume of a service or product needed not to lose money.

Business plan A complex financial document that determines the financial feasibility of an enterprise; includes a break-even analysis, a cash flow analysis, and a pro forma financial statement.

Cash-flow analysis The pattern of cash outlay and cash receivables that will determine how much financial investment is needed to seed a project.

Charter A formal directive for action; an official mandate supported by the leadership or governance of an organization.

Consensus A group arriving at agreement about the best decision after entering into a dialogue.

Content The substance of cultural themes.

Critical thinking A dynamic skill that requires sound problem identification, a broad perspective, adequate data, and the ability to suspend judgment based on one's biases; includes thinking about one's thinking.

Cultural listening A skill used by organizational development specialists that attunes to the rituals, symbolic gestures, symbols, language, and thought processes of an organization that relate to its culture.

Customer focus An approach that centers all activities and priorities of the organization on the customers of the services or products.

Customers All the people whom the work must satisfy.

Delegation The granting of authority to team members who share responsibility and accountability for task completion.

Dialogue A constructive discussion in which all participants actively listen, suspend judgment, and interact without prejudice as to the conclusion.

Differentiation Various cultures that are apparent across subunits of an organization.

Digout A Japanese term for a manager's helping staff find improvements that will make their jobs easier.

Diversity An organizational characteristic that seeks out new views and encourages free thinking and risk taking. It embraces people from diverse backgrounds and training and finds ways to break down organizational barriers to these people's freely engaging in innovation.

Driving forces External or internal demands that prompt change.

Empowerment An inward feeling of power to do one's job without outside influence; the strength to question issues central to the job.

Ethical leadership Leadership driven from a life philosophy that is consistent, moral, and centered.

External integration The extent to which external cultures and communication are in concert with the organization's culture.

Financial plan A complete projection of the costs, necessary volume to break even, and operating and capital budgets related to a proposed service or product.

Focus group A gathering of customers for the purpose of providing feedback on a topic, service, or problem.

Group think When individuals of a group are so bonded that they refrain from expressing their opinions due to the need to belong to the group.

Guiding principles Broad concepts based on organizational beliefs that will serve as a template for major change initiatives.

Holusion A multilayered, three-dimensional picture that must be viewed closely and without focusing on the picture itself; a visual parable for looking at the big picture.

Indicators Measures that are predetermined to gauge an aspect of quality.

Influence A dynamic process that does not seek to control but to set in place an interdependence that fosters cooperation.

Innovation To change constantly in many ways; to try new things in an effort to improve processes and outcomes; to question basic practices and enter into opposing frames of reference.

Integration A single culture operating within a complex structure.

Integrative structure A form that communicates interdependency and dynamic exchange among multiple points; demonstrates diversity with unity.

Internal integration Substructures within the organization have compatible cultures.

Job design focused A system that revolves around job descriptions at the expense of flexibility.

Kaizen A Japanese term meaning "continuously improving in small ways."

Kaleidoscope thinking Looking at a problem in a way that allows new patterns to emerge because basic assumptions were challenged.

Knowledge worker A worker who must exercise critical thinking and complex mental operations in the process of performing the duties of the job.

Learning organization People within the organization constantly seek new insights and new ways of framing their challenges so that collective aspirations are set free to modify behavior in a planned way.

Leverage Receiving the best result from well-focused actions.

Market analysis An investigation of data measuring desired aspects of the marketing environment for the purpose of improving an organization's marketing decisions.

Mediator Key people who amplify, modify, and organize stimuli that occur in everyday experiences with the vision of affecting behavior toward core goals of the organization.

Metaphor A simple image used to convey a complex issue or concept.

Needs analysis An in-depth evaluation of the anticipated efficacy of an endeavor that includes justifying need and utilization of the service, as well as financial feasibility.

Organizational climate Individual perceptions about an organization.

Organizational commitment The extent to which an organization will continue change efforts in spite of political, cultural, or financial challenges.

Organizational culture Shared values and beliefs that underlie continuing interactions within an organization.

Organizational development A discipline that facilitates the alignment of an organization's systems with its visions, goals, and desired outcomes.

Organizational dialogue Honest and direct communication that is non-hierarchical and centers on listening to and responding to others rather than only presenting one's own thoughts.

Organizational readiness A characteristic of the organization that indicates the culture supports change and innovation. Individuals can tolerate ambiguity inherent in change, and there is sufficient trust to ensure risk taking needed for true innovation.

Outcome An aspect of evaluation that concentrates on intended and unintended results that occur subsequent to an activity.

Paradigm A personal worldview about a concept based on historical, cultural, and/or value-driven ideals that drives how things get done.

Partnership An organizational philosophy that embraces all customers as full partners in the work of the organization.

Patient-focused care delivery Care systems that center on patients, not the caregivers. Simplicity, innovation, quality, and stewardship are central to the patient-focused care ideal.

Patriarchy An organizational philosophy that is top down and autocratic in design.

Personal mastery The ability to focus, clarify, and deepen a personal vision as well as to see reality objectively. To refine one's skills to the point of expertise.

Power A control over others that exacts a desired outcome due to implied or specified consequences.

Process A series of actions focused on a specific outcome. Also defined from an interpersonal perspective as the act of working through an issue or, an aspect of evaluation that concentrates on how care is provided and ways to improve systems and care delivery.

Pro forma Financial statements that propose the financial position of a project within a specified time period, generally in fiscal year projections.

Project An organizational strategy to achieve change through specific goal attainment within a limited time frame by targeting resources.

Quick changeover Maximizing efficiency of the internal steps of a process by having the external steps prepared ahead of time.

Reality What an individual or group perceives to be the characteristics, makeup, or traits of their experience; what a person believes to be true in his or her lived experience.

Redesign The act of reinventing practices and processes in an effort to improve care continuously; change of a fundamental nature.

Restraining forces Internal and external forces that resist change. This concept is part of assessing the force field of driving and restraining forces in relationship to change.

Rituals Formalized ways in which an organization celebrates landmark events; historically significant acts that are maintained and valued as representing the values or culture of the organization.

Sacred cows Revered images of an organization where interference is taboo.

Self-managed teams A team that controls its operations and outputs, including setting goals, measuring success, evaluating team members, and selecting the leader.

Sentinel events Key events that are exceptions to standards of care. These must be noted quickly because they trigger adverse outcomes.

Shared governance A management philosophy that includes staff in decisions that affect their practice. Generally there are staff councils that have specific operating responsibilities and provide needed structure.

Shared leadership A management philosophy that encourages leadership growth in staff on a multidisciplinary level. It may take a form similar to shared governance in that multidisciplinary staff councils may address operational needs in a structured manner.

Stewardship Accountability for one's productivity, ability to conserve organizational resources, and to be directly responsive to customers without external motivation.

Structure An aspect of evaluation that concentrates on organizational properties or physical attributes of care.

Symbol An icon, emblem, or representation of something abstract that has meaning within the organization.

Synergy A state where people, working together optimally, are able to increase their collective effectiveness.

Systems redesign focused A redesign approach that addresses change from a systems perspective.

System thinking Awareness by the individual or group that their experience is dynamic and nonlinear. Causation is not a cause and effect but multiple, diverse, known, and unknown.

Taboo Organizational must nots.

Technical change Modification of the organization's usual activities.

Thresholds The level of acceptable performance that is predetermined for all indicators of quality.

Total quality management (TQM) A quality-oriented discipline that prescribes specific steps to improve processes of work.

Transformation Change of a fundamental nature that affects the very paradigms and culture that undergird an organization.

Transformational leadership Leaders who can foster alignment between individuals and the organization's goals in a way that profoundly changes the organization.

Transitional change An alteration of goals but not how the goals are achieved.

Index

f indicates information that can be found in a figure.
t indicates information that can be found in a table.